ELASTICSEARCH 8 IN A

REAL-WORLD SEARCH SOLUTION

OLIVER LUCAS JR

TABLE OF CONTENTS

Chapter 1

Chapter 2

Chapter 3

Chapter 4

Chapter 5

Chapter 6

Chapter 7

Chapter 8

Chapter 9

Chapter 10

preface

If you're looking to build powerful search applications with Elasticsearch 8, this book is for you. *Elasticsearch 8 in Action: Real-World Search Solutions* will equip you with the knowledge and skills to:

Index and manage data efficiently.

Craft complex queries to extract valuable insights.

Implement filtering, faceting, and other advanced search features.

Optimize performance for speed and scalability.

Secure your Elasticsearch cluster.

Through practical examples and clear explanations, this book will empower you to master Elasticsearch 8 and build real-world search solutions that meet the demands of today's data-driven world.

Chapter 1

Getting Started with Elasticsearch 8

Let's break down "1.1 Choosing Your Installation Method" in even more detail, as it's the crucial first step in setting up Elasticsearch. This section should equip the reader with the knowledge to select the best installation approach for their needs and operating system.

1.1 Choosing Your Installation Method

This section should begin by explaining that there are several ways to install Elasticsearch, each with its own advantages and disadvantages. It should emphasize that the best method depends on factors like the user's operating system, technical expertise, and intended use case (development, testing, or production).

1.1.1 Installing from a `.tar.gz` archive (Linux/macOS)

This is often the recommended approach for Linux and macOS, especially for production environments, as it gives the most control over the installation.

Downloading the Archive: Provide a clear link to the official Elasticsearch download page on the Elastic website. Explain how to choose the correct version (8.x.x) and the `.tar.gz` archive.

Extracting the Archive: Show the command to extract the archive using `tar -xzf elasticsearch-*.tar.gz`. Explain how to navigate to the extracted directory.

Setting Environment Variables (Optional but Recommended): Explain how to set the `JAVA_HOME` environment variable if Java isn't already configured correctly. This ensures Elasticsearch uses the correct Java version.

Directory Structure: Briefly explain the important directories within the extracted folder, such as `bin` (for executables), `config` (for configuration files), and `data` (for data storage).

Starting Elasticsearch: Show the command to start Elasticsearch using `./bin/elasticsearch`. Explain how to run it in the background using `nohup` or systemd (for production).

1.1.2 Installing with Docker

Docker is an excellent option for quick setup, testing, and containerized deployments.

Prerequisites: Mention that Docker needs to be installed on the user's system. Provide links to the official Docker installation instructions.

Pulling the Elasticsearch Image: Show the command to pull the official Elasticsearch Docker image from Docker Hub: `docker pull docker.elastic.co/elasticsearch/elasticsearch:8.x.x`.

Running the Container: Provide a clear example of the `docker run` command, including important options:

`-p 9200:9200 -p 9300:9300`: Exposing the HTTP and transport ports.

`-e "discovery.type=single-node"`: Running Elasticsearch in single-node mode for development.

`-e "ES_JAVA_OPTS=-Xms512m -Xmx512m"`: Setting the JVM heap size.

`-v esdata:/usr/share/elasticsearch/data`: Mounting a volume for persistent data storage.

Accessing Elasticsearch: Explain how to access Elasticsearch through `localhost:9200` in a web browser or using `curl`.

Docker Compose (Optional): Briefly introduce Docker Compose as a way to manage multi-container applications, including Elasticsearch and Kibana.

1.1.3 Installing on Windows

The installation on Windows uses a `.zip` archive.

Downloading the Archive: Provide a link to the download page and instructions for downloading the `.zip`archive.

Extracting the Archive: Explain how to extract the archive using File Explorer or a similar tool.

Starting Elasticsearch: Show how to start Elasticsearch by running `elasticsearch.bat` from the `bin` directory.

Windows-Specific Considerations: Mention any Windows-specific considerations, such as setting environment variables or dealing with file paths.

1.1.4 Installing with Package Managers (apt, yum, etc.)

This method is convenient for Linux distributions that use package managers.

Adding the Elastic Repository: Explain how to add the Elastic repository to the system's package manager. Provide specific instructions for different distributions (Debian/Ubuntu, RHEL/CentOS).

Installing Elasticsearch: Show the command to install Elasticsearch using `apt-get install elasticsearch` or `yum install elasticsearch`.

Starting Elasticsearch: Explain how to start the Elasticsearch service using `systemctl start elasticsearch` or `service elasticsearch start`.

Configuration Files: Explain the default locations of the configuration files.

Key improvements for this detailed explanation:

More Specific Commands: Providing the exact commands users need to run.

Explanation of Options: Explaining the purpose of each option used in the commands.

Emphasis on Best Practices: Highlighting best practices, like setting environment variables and using Docker volumes.

Operating System Specificity: Giving tailored instructions for each operating system.

By providing this level of detail, you ensure that readers of all skill levels can successfully install Elasticsearch and begin working with it. Remember to use clear language, code blocks, and screenshots to make the process as easy as possible.

Let's break down the "Understanding the Elasticsearch Ecosystem (Kibana, Beats, Logstash)" subtitle. This section is crucial for giving readers context about how Elasticsearch fits within the broader Elastic Stack (formerly known as the ELK stack).

1.2 Understanding the Elasticsearch Ecosystem (Kibana, Beats, Logstash)

This section should explain that Elasticsearch is not just a standalone search engine but is part of a powerful suite of tools designed for data ingestion, analysis, and visualization.[1]

Subsections:

1.2.1 Introducing the Elastic Stack: Start by formally introducing the Elastic Stack (or the Elastic ecosystem) as a collection of open-source tools built around Elasticsearch. Explain that these tools work together seamlessly to provide a comprehensive solution for various use cases like search, logging, security analytics, and business intelligence.

1.2.2 Kibana: Visualizing and Exploring Your Data:

Purpose: Explain that Kibana is the visualization and exploration tool for the Elastic Stack. It provides a web interface for creating dashboards, visualizations (charts, graphs, maps), and exploring data stored in Elasticsearch.[2]

Key Features: Highlight some key features:

Data Visualization: Creating various types of charts and graphs to represent data.

Dashboards: Combining multiple visualizations into interactive dashboards.[3]

Discover: Interactively exploring data using a query interface.

Dev Tools: A console for interacting directly with the Elasticsearch API.[4]

Canvas: Creating pixel-perfect presentations and reports.[5]

Connection to Elasticsearch: Explain how Kibana connects to Elasticsearch to retrieve data and how it allows users to query and filter that data.

1.2.3 Beats: Shipping Your Data:

Purpose: Explain that Beats are lightweight shippers that collect data from various sources and forward it to Elasticsearch or Logstash.[6]

Types of Beats: Introduce some of the most common Beats:

Filebeat: For collecting log files.

Metricbeat: For collecting system and service metrics.

Packetbeat: For network packet analysis.

Winlogbeat: For collecting Windows event logs.

Heartbeat: For monitoring the uptime of services.

How Beats Work: Briefly explain how Beats work by configuring them to monitor specific data sources and then sending that data to Elasticsearch or Logstash.

1.2.4 Logstash: Processing and Enriching Your Data:

Purpose: Explain that Logstash is a data processing pipeline that can ingest data from various sources, transform it, and then send it to Elasticsearch.

Key Features: Highlight some key features:

Input Plugins: For receiving data from different sources (e.g., files, logs, databases).[8]

Filter Plugins: For transforming and enriching data (e.g., parsing logs, adding GeoIP information).

Output Plugins: For sending data to different destinations (e.g., Elasticsearch, other databases).[9]

Use Cases: Give examples of how Logstash is used, such as parsing complex log formats, enriching data with external information, and routing data to different destinations.

Relationship with Beats: Explain how Beats often send data to Logstash for further processing before it's indexed in Elasticsearch. This is especially useful for complex data transformations.

1.2.5 Choosing the Right Tool: Briefly discuss when to use Beats versus Logstash. Generally:

Beats: Simpler data collection, lightweight, for straightforward data shipping.

Logstash: Complex data processing, transformations, enrichment, for more advanced data pipelines.[10]

Visual Aid:

It would be very beneficial to include a diagram illustrating the relationship between Elasticsearch, Kibana, Beats, and Logstash. This visual representation will help readers understand how these components fit together. A simple diagram could show data flowing from Beats and/or other sources into Logstash (optional), then into Elasticsearch, and finally being visualized in Kibana.

By covering these points, you'll provide a solid foundation for understanding the broader context of Elasticsearch and its role within the Elastic Stack. This will be invaluable as readers progress through the book and learn how to use these tools together to build powerful solutions.

Let's break down the "Basic Concepts: Documents, Indices, and Shards" subtitle. This is foundational knowledge for anyone working with Elasticsearch.

1.3 Basic Concepts: Documents, Indices, and Shards

This section should explain the core data structures and how they relate to each other. Use analogies and clear examples to make these concepts easy to grasp.

Subsections:

1.3.1 Documents: The Unit of Data:

Definition: Explain that a document is the basic unit of information in Elasticsearch. It's a JSON (JavaScript Object Notation) object that contains key-value pairs.

Analogy: Compare a document to a row in a relational database table or a document in a NoSQL database like MongoDB.

Example: Provide a simple example of a JSON document representing a product:

JSON

```
{
  "product_id": "123",
  "name": "Awesome T-Shirt",
  "description": "A comfortable and stylish t-shirt.",
```

```
  "price": 19.99,
  "color": "Blue"
}
```

Key-Value Pairs: Explain that each piece of data within a document is represented as a key-value pair. The key is the name of the field, and the value is the data itself.

Data Types: Briefly mention that Elasticsearch supports various data types, such as text, numbers, dates, booleans, and geo-points. This will be covered in more detail in the chapter on indexing.

1.3.2 Indices: Organizing Your Documents:

Definition: Explain that an index is a collection of documents that have similar characteristics. It's like a table in a relational database or a collection in MongoDB.

Analogy: Use the analogy of a library. An index is like a section of the library (e.g., "Science Fiction," "History"), and the documents are the books within that section.

Example: Explain that you might have an index called "products" to store product information, an index called "logs" to store log data, or an index called "users" to store user information.

Naming Conventions: Briefly mention index naming conventions (lowercase, no spaces, use underscores or hyphens).

1.3.3 Shards: Scaling Your Index:

Definition: Explain that an index can be divided into multiple parts called shards. Shards are the units of distribution and scaling in Elasticsearch.

Analogy: Continue the library analogy. Shards are like different copies of the same section of the library, distributed across different branches.

Primary Shards and Replicas: Explain the difference between primary shards and replica shards:

Primary Shards: The original shards of the index. They are required for indexing and searching.

Replica Shards: Copies of the primary shards. They provide redundancy and improve search performance.

Benefits of Sharding: Explain the benefits of sharding:

Horizontal Scaling: Allows you to distribute your data across multiple nodes in a cluster, enabling you to handle large amounts of data.

Improved Performance: Distributing search queries across multiple shards can significantly improve search speed.

High Availability: If one node fails, the replica shards can take over, ensuring that your data remains accessible.

Shard Allocation: Briefly mention how Elasticsearch automatically distributes shards across the nodes in a cluster.

1.3.4 Relationships Between Documents, Indices, and Shards:

Summary: Clearly summarize the relationship: Documents are stored within indices, and indices are divided into shards.

Diagram: A simple diagram showing documents within an index, and the index being divided into primary and replica shards, would be extremely helpful here.

Example Diagram (Conceptual):

```
+-----------------+     +-----------------+     +-----------------+
|  Index (e.g.,   |---->|  Shard 1 (P)    |---->|  Node 1         |
|  "products")    |     +-----------------+     +-----------------+
+-----------------+     +-----------------+     +-----------------+
|                 |     |  Shard 2 (P)    |---->|  Node 2         |
|                 |     +-----------------+     +-----------------+
|                 |     +-----------------+     +-----------------+
|                 |     |  Shard 1 (R)    |---->|  Node 3         |
|                 |     +-----------------+     +-----------------+
|                 |     +-----------------+     +-----------------+
|                 |     |  Shard 2 (R)    |---->|  Node 4         |
|                 |     +-----------------+     +-----------------+
+-----------------+
     ^
     |
+-----+-----+
| Document 1 |
+-----+-----+
| Document 2 |
+-----+-----+
|   ...     |
+-----+-----+
```

By explaining these fundamental concepts clearly and using analogies and visuals, you will prepare your readers for the more advanced topics that follow.

Chapter 2

Indexing Your Data

Let's break down the "Mapping Your Data for Optimal Search" subtitle, which is crucial for effectively using Elasticsearch. Mapping defines how Elasticsearch understands and indexes your data.

2.1 Mapping Your Data for Optimal Search

This section should explain what mapping is, why it's important, and how to define mappings for different data types.

Subsections:

2.1.1 What is Mapping?

Definition: Explain that mapping is the process of defining how a document and its fields should be stored and indexed in Elasticsearch. It's like defining the schema of a table in a relational database.

Purpose: Explain why mapping is essential:

Data Type Definition: It tells Elasticsearch the data type of each field (e.g., text, keyword, date, integer).

Indexing Control: It controls how the data is indexed, which affects search performance and capabilities.

Search Optimization: Correct mapping cansignificantly improve search relevance and efficiency.

Dynamic Mapping: Explain that Elasticsearch can dynamically create mappings based on the first document indexed. However, it's generally recommended to define explicit mappings for better control.

2.1.2 Core Data Types:

`text`: Explain that this type is used for full-text search. It's analyzed by default, meaning the text is broken down into individual words (tokens) for indexing.

Example: Product descriptions, blog posts, articles.

Analyzers: Briefly introduce the concept of analyzers, which are used to process text fields. Default analyzers are usually sufficient but can be customized.

`keyword`: Explain that this type is used for exact matching, filtering, sorting, and aggregations. It's not analyzed.

Example: Product IDs, tags, categories.

`date`: Explain that this type is used for storing dates and times. It allows for date-based queries and aggregations.

Formats: Mention the importance of specifying date formats to ensure proper parsing.

`integer`, `long`, `float`, `double`: Explain these numeric types for storing numbers.

`boolean`: Explain this type for storing true/false values.

`geo_point`: Explain this type for storing geographical coordinates (latitude and longitude).

Other Types: Briefly mention other types like `ip`, `binary`, `object`, and `nested` (which will be discussed later if relevant).

2.1.3 Defining Explicit Mappings:

Mapping Structure: Show the basic structure of a mapping definition in JSON:

JSON

```
PUT my_index
{
  "mappings": {
    "properties": {
      "product_id": { "type": "keyword" },
      "name": { "type": "text" },
      "description": { "type": "text" },
      "price": { "type": "float" },
            "created_at": { "type": "date", "format": "yyyy-MM-dd
HH:mm:ss" }
    }
  }
}
```

properties: Explain that the properties section defines the fields within the documents.

Field Names: Explain that field names should be lowercase and use underscores or hyphens.

type: Explain how to specify the data type for each field.

Other Mapping Parameters: Briefly introduce other important mapping parameters, such as:

index: Controls whether a field is indexed for searching.

`analyzer`: Specifies the analyzer to use for text fields.

`format` (for dates): Specifies the date format.

2.1.4 Updating Mappings:

Limitations: Explain that you cannot change the mapping of an existing field. You would need to create a new index with the updated mapping and reindex your data.

`_mapping` API: Show how to view the mapping of an existing index using the `_mapping` API:

Bash

GET my_index/_mappin

2.1.5 Practical Examples:

Provide several practical examples of mapping definitions for different use cases, such as e-commerce products, blog posts, or log data.

By covering these points, you'll give readers a solid understanding of how to map their data effectively for optimal search performance in Elasticsearch. Emphasize the importance of planning the mapping upfront to avoid issues later on.

Let's delve into "Bulk Indexing for Performance," a crucial topic for efficient data ingestion into Elasticsearch.

2.2 Bulk Indexing for Performance

This section should explain why bulk indexing is important and how to use the Bulk API effectively.

Subsections:

2.2.1 Why Bulk Indexing?

Performance Bottleneck of Individual Requests: Explain that sending individual indexing requests for each document is inefficient due to the overhead of network communication and processing for each request.

Benefits of Bulk Requests: Explain how bulk requests significantly improve indexing performance by sending multiple operations (index, create, update, delete) in a single request. This reduces network round trips and allows Elasticsearch to optimize the indexing process.

Analogy: Compare sending individual letters through the mail (slow) to sending a package containing multiple letters (fast).

2.2.2 The Bulk API Format:

Structure: Explain the structure of a bulk request. It's a newline-delimited JSON format with two lines per operation:

Action and Metadata Line: Specifies the operation (index, create, update, delete) and metadata like the index and document ID.

Document Source Line: Contains the JSON document to be indexed.

Example: Provide a clear example of a bulk request:

JSON

POST _bulk

```
{"index": {"_index": "products", "_id": "1"}}
{"name": "Product A", "description": "Description of Product A"}
{"create": {"_index": "products", "_id": "2"}}
{"name": "Product B", "description": "Description of Product B"}
{"update": {"_index": "products", "_id": "1"}}
{"doc": {"description": "Updated description of Product A"}}
{"delete": {"_index": "products", "_id": "3"}}
```

Explanation of Actions: Explain each action:

index: Creates a new document or replaces an existing one if the ID already exists.

create: Creates a new document. Fails if a document with the same ID already exists.

update: Updates an existing document.

delete: Deletes a document.

2.2.3 Sending Bulk Requests:

Using curl: Show how to send bulk requests using curl:

Bash
```
curl -X POST -H "Content-Type: application/x-ndjson" -d @bulk_data.json http://localhost:9200/_bulk
```

Where bulk_data.json contains the bulk request data.

Client Libraries: Mention that most Elasticsearch client libraries provide convenient methods for creating and sending bulk requests. Provide brief examples using a popular client library (e.g., the official Elasticsearch client for Python or Java).

2.2.4 Handling Bulk Responses:

Response Format: Explain the format of the bulk response, which contains information about the success or failure of each operation.

Error Handling: Explain how to handle errors in the bulk response. The response contains an errors field that indicates if any operations failed. It's crucial to check this field and handle errors appropriately (e.g., retry failed operations).

Example Response: Provide an example of a bulk response with some errors:

JSON

```
{
  "took": 10,
  "errors": true,
  "items": [
    {
      "index": {
        "_index": "products",
        "_id": "1",
        "result": "created",
        "status": 201
      }
    },
    {
      "create": {
        "_index": "products",
        "_id": "2",
        "error": {
          "type": "version_conflict_engine_exception",
          "reason": "[2]: version conflict, document already exists"
        },
```

```
    "status": 409
   }
  }
 ]
}
```

2.2.5 Optimizing Bulk Indexing:

Batch Size: Explain the importance of choosing an appropriate batch size. Too small batches negate the benefits of bulk indexing, while too large batches can consume excessive memory. Recommend starting with a batch size of 1000-5000 documents and adjusting based on testing.

Indexing Rate: Explain how to monitor the indexing rate and adjust the batch size or other settings to achieve optimal performance.

Number of Workers/Threads: When using client libraries, discuss the use of multiple workers or threads to send bulk requests concurrently.

By covering these points, you'll equip your readers with the knowledge and skills to efficiently index large amounts of data into Elasticsearch using the Bulk API. This is essential for building high-performance search applications. Remember to use clear examples, code snippets, and explanations to make the concepts easy to understand.

Let's break down "Handling Different Data Types (Text, Numbers, Dates, Geo)," a crucial section for effective data modeling in Elasticsearch.

2.3 Handling Different Data Types (Text, Numbers, Dates, Geo)

This section should provide a deeper dive into how to handle various data types in Elasticsearch, building upon the introduction to data types in the mapping section.

Subsections:

2.3.1 Text Data:

`text` **vs.** `keyword` **Revisited:** Reinforce the difference: `text` is for full-text search (analyzed), while `keyword`is for exact matching, filtering, sorting, and aggregations (not analyzed).

Analyzers in Detail: Explain analyzers more thoroughly:

Character Filters: Preprocess the text by removing or modifying characters (e.g., HTML tags).

Tokenizers: Break the text into individual words (tokens).

Token Filters: Modify the tokens (e.g., lowercase, stemming, stop word removal).

Standard Analyzer: Explain the default `standard` analyzer and its components.

Other Built-in Analyzers: Introduce other common analyzers like `whitespace`, `simple`, `stop`, `keyword`, **and** `stemming` analyzers, and explain their use cases.

Custom Analyzers: Briefly introduce the concept of creating custom analyzers by combining different character filters, tokenizers, and token filters. This will be covered in more detail in a later chapter if appropriate.

Example Mapping: Show examples of mapping text fields with different analyzers:

JSON

```
PUT my_index
{
  "mappings": {
    "properties": {
      "title": { "type": "text", "analyzer": "standard" },
      "description": { "type": "text", "analyzer": "whitespace" },
      "tags": { "type": "keyword" }
    }
  }
}
```

2.3.2 Numeric Data:

Data Types: Explain the different numeric types:

byte, short, integer, long: **For whole numbers.**

float, double: **For floating-point numbers.**

half_float: **For smaller floating-point numbers (less precision, smaller storage).**

scaled_float: **For fixed-point numbers.**

Choosing the Right Type: Explain how to choose the appropriate numeric type based on the range and precision of the data.

Indexing and Searching: Explain how numeric data is indexed and how to perform range queries and aggregations on numeric fields.

Example Mapping:

JSON

```
PUT my_index
{
  "mappings": {
    "properties": {
      "price": { "type": "float" },
      "quantity": { "type": "integer" }
    }
  }
}
```

2.3.3 Date Data:
`date` **Type:** Explain the `date` type and its importance for storing dates and times.

Date Formats: Emphasize the importance of specifying date formats using the `format` parameter. Provide examples of common date formats:

`yyyy-MM-dd`
`yyyy-MM-dd HH:mm:ss`
`epoch_millis` (milliseconds since the epoch)
`epoch_second` (seconds since the epoch)

Date Math: Briefly introduce date math for querying data within specific time ranges (e.g., "now-1d" for the last day).

Example Mapping:

JSON

```
PUT my_index
{
  "mappings": {
   "properties": {
         "created_at": { "type": "date", "format": "yyyy-MM-dd
HH:mm:ss||epoch_millis" }
   }
  }
}
```

2.3.4 Geospatial Data:

`geo_point` **Type:** Explain the `geo_point` type for storing geographical coordinates (latitude and longitude).

Formats: Explain the different formats for representing geo-points:

String: `"lat,lon"` (e.g., "40.715,-74.008")

Object: `{"lat": 40.715, "lon": -74.008}`

Array: `[-74.008, 40.715]` (longitude first)

Geo Queries: Briefly introduce geo queries like `geo_distance`, `geo_bounding_box`, and `geo_polygon`. These will be covered in more detail in a later chapter.

Example Mapping:
JSON

```
PUT my_index
{
  "mappings": {
    "properties": {
      "location": { "type": "geo_point" }
    }
  }
}
```

2.3.5 Other Data Types (Brief Overview):

Briefly mention other data types like boolean, ip, binary, object, and nested. Explain when these types are useful and that they will be covered if relevant in more advanced chapters.

By providing this detailed explanation of data types and their mapping options, you'll give your readers the tools they need to effectively model their data in Elasticsearch for optimal search and analysis. Remember to include clear examples and code snippets to illustrate the concepts.

Chapter 3

Basic Search Operations

Let's break down "Understanding Query DSL (Domain Specific Language)," a core concept for searching in Elasticsearch.

3.1 Understanding Query DSL (Domain Specific Language)

This section should introduce the Query DSL, explaining its structure and purpose, and laying the groundwork for more complex queries later.

Subsections:

3.1.1 What is the Query DSL?

Definition: Explain that the Query DSL (Domain Specific Language) is a JSON-based language used to define search queries in Elasticsearch.

Purpose: Explain why the Query DSL is used:

Flexibility: It provides a powerful and flexible way to express complex search criteria.

Structure: It provides a structured way to define queries, making them easier to understand and maintain.

Performance: It allows Elasticsearch to optimize query execution.

Contrast with Simple Query Strings: Briefly contrast the Query DSL with simple query strings (e.g., using the `q` parameter in a URL). Explain that while simple queries are convenient for basic searches, the Query DSL is necessary for more advanced scenarios.

3.1.2 Basic Query Structure:

Query Context vs. Filter Context: Explain the crucial difference between query context and filter context:

Query Context: Used for scoring documents based on relevance. Queries in this context calculate a `_score` for each matching document.

Filter Context: Used for filtering documents based on a condition. Filters do not calculate a `_score`. They simply include or exclude documents. Filters are generally faster than queries in query context.

JSON Structure: Show the basic JSON structure of a query:

JSON

```
GET my_index/_search
{
  "query": {
    "match": {
      "field_name": "search_term"
    }
  }
}
```

`query` **Clause:** Explain that the `query` clause contains the actual query definition.

Query Types: Briefly introduce some basic query types (e.g., `match`, `term`, `range`) that will be explained in more detail in subsequent sections.

3.1.3 Match Query:

Purpose: Explain that the `match` query is the standard query for performing full-text searches on `text` fields.

Analysis: Explain that the `match` query analyzes the search term before querying, just like the field is analyzed during indexing.

Example:
JSON

```
GET my_index/_search
{
  "query": {
    "match": {
      "description": "quick brown fox"
    }
  }
}
```

Operators (OR, AND): Explain how to use operators like `or` (default) and `and` to combine multiple search terms:
JSON

```
GET my_index/_search
{
  "query": {
```

```json
  "match": {
    "description": {
      "query": "quick brown fox",
      "operator": "and"
    }
  }
 }
}
```

3.1.4 Term Query:

Purpose: Explain that the `term` query is used for exact matching on `keyword` fields or other non-analyzed fields.

No Analysis: Emphasize that the `term` query does *not* analyze the search term.
Example:
JSON

```json
GET my_index/_search
{
  "query": {
    "term": {
      "product_id": "123"
    }
  }
}
```

3.1.5 Range Query:

Purpose: Explain that the `range` query is used to search for values within a specific range.
Operators: Explain the range operators:

gt: Greater than

gte: Greater than or equal to

lt: Less than

lte: Less than or equal to

Example:

JSON

```
GET my_index/_search
{
  "query": {
    "range": {
      "price": {
        "gte": 10,
        "lte": 20
      }
    }
  }
}
```

3.1.6 Boolean Queries (Combining Queries):

bool Query: Explain that the bool query is used to combine multiple queries using boolean logic.

Clauses: Explain the different clauses within a bool query:

must: Documents must match these queries (AND).

should: Documents should match these queries (OR). Increases the score if matched.

must_not: Documents must *not* match these queries (NOT).

filter: Filters documents based on a condition. Does not affect the score.
Example:

JSON

```
GET my_index/_search
{
  "query": {
    "bool": {
      "must": [
        { "match": { "description": "t-shirt" } }
      ],
      "filter": [
        { "term": { "color": "blue" } }
      ]
    }
  }
}
```

By covering these points, you'll provide a solid foundation for understanding the Query DSL and how to construct basic queries in Elasticsearch. This will prepare readers for the more advanced query techniques that will be covered in later chapters. Remember to use clear examples and explanations to make the concepts easy to grasp.

Let's break down "Performing Full-Text Searches," a core function of Elasticsearch and a key topic for your book.

3.2 Performing Full-Text Searches

This section should delve deeper into how Elasticsearch handles full-text search, building upon the introduction to the `match` query in the previous section.

Subsections:

3.2.1 The `match` Query in Detail:

Analysis Process: Reiterate that the `match` query analyzes the query string before searching, using the same analyzer used for indexing the field. This ensures that searches are performed on the indexed terms, not the raw text.

Operators (OR, AND, Minimum Should Match): Explain the different operators that can be used with the `match` query:

`or` **(default):** Documents that contain any of the search terms will match.

`and`: Documents must contain all of the search terms to match.

`minimum_should_match`: Allows you to specify a minimum number of terms that must match. This is useful for handling optional terms. Explain how to use both absolute values (e.g., 2) and percentages (e.g., 50%).

Example:

JSON

```
GET my_index/_search
{
  "query": {
    "match": {
```

```
  "description": {
    "query": "quick brown fox jumps",
      "minimum_should_match": "75%" // At least 3 of the 4 terms
must match
    }
   }
  }
}
```

Fuzziness: Introduce the `fuzziness` parameter, which allows for fuzzy matching (matching terms that are similar to the search term, even with typos). Explain different fuzziness settings:

0: Exact match only.

1: Allow one edit (insertion, deletion, substitution).

2: Allow two edits.

AUTO: Automatically determine the fuzziness based on the length of the term.

Example:
JSON

```
GET my_index/_search
{
  "query": {
    "match": {
      "description": {
        "query": "broen",
        "fuzziness": "AUTO"
      }
    }
```

```
  }
}
```

Zero Terms Query: Explain the `zero_terms_query` parameter which controls the behavior when all terms are removed by the analyzer (for instance when using stop words). Options are `none` (default) and `all`.

3.2.2 Phrase Matching (`match_phrase`):

Purpose: Explain that the `match_phrase` query is used to search for exact phrases (sequences of words).

Slop: Introduce the `slop` parameter, which allows for words to be out of order by a specified number of positions. This is useful for handling slight variations in phrasing.
Example:
JSON

```
GET my_index/_search
{
  "query": {
    "match_phrase": {
      "description": {
        "query": "quick fox",
        "slop": 1 // Allows "quick brown fox" to match
      }
    }
  }
}
```

3.2.3 Phrase Prefix Matching (`match_phrase_prefix`):

Purpose: Explain that the `match_phrase_prefix` query is similar to `match_phrase` but allows for prefix matching on the last term in the phrase. This is useful for autocompletion or "type-ahead" search.

Example:
JSON

```
GET my_index/_search
{
  "query": {
    "match_phrase_prefix": {
      "description": {
        "query": "quick bro" // Matches "quick brown", "quick bronze",
etc.
      }
    }
  }
}
```

3.2.4 Multi-Match Query:

Purpose: Explain that the `multi_match` query allows you to search multiple fields with a single query.

`fields` **Parameter:** Explain how to specify the fields to search using the `fields` parameter

`type` **Parameter:** Introduce the `type` parameter and its different options:

`best_fields` (default): Finds the best matching field for each term.

`most_fields`: Combines the scores from all matching fields.

`cross_fields`: Treats multiple fields as if they were one large field.

`phrase` and `phrase_prefix`: Apply phrase matching or phrase prefix matching across multiple fields.
Example:

JSON

```
GET my_index/_search
{
  "query": {
   "multi_match": {
     "query": "quick brown",
     "fields": ["title", "description"],
     "type": "best_fields"
   }
  }
}
```

By covering these points, you'll equip your readers with a strong understanding of how to perform effective full-text searches in Elasticsearch using various query types and parameters. Remember to use clear examples, code snippets, and explanations to illustrate the concepts. This section is critical for anyone building search-driven applications.

Let's break down "Filtering and Sorting Results," which is essential for refining search results in Elasticsearch.

3.3 Filtering and Sorting Results

This section should explain how to use filters to narrow down search results and how to sort them based on different criteria.

Subsections:

3.3.1 Filtering vs. Querying:

Reiterating the Difference: Reinforce the key difference between queries (query context) and filters (filter context). Queries calculate a relevance score (`_score`), while filters simply include or exclude documents without affecting the score.

Performance Implications: Explain that filters are generally faster than queries because they don't need to calculate scores. Elasticsearch can also cache filters for even better performance.

When to Use Filters: Explain that filters are best used for:

Filtering based on exact values (e.g., category, color, status).

Filtering based on ranges (e.g., price, date).

Filtering based on boolean conditions.

Filtering based on geo-spatial criteria.

3.3.2 Using Filters with the `filter` Context:

`bool` **Query with** `filter` **Clause:** Explain that filters are used within the `filter` clause of a `bool` query.

Example:

JSON

GET my_index/_search

```
{
  "query": {
    "bool": {
      "must": { "match": { "description": "t-shirt" } },
      "filter": [
        { "term": { "color": "blue" } },
        { "range": { "price": { "gte": 10, "lte": 20 } } }
      ]
    }
  }
}
```

Common Filter Types: Explain some common filter types:

`term` **Filter:** For exact matching on a single value (similar to the `term` query).

`terms` **Filter:** For matching on multiple values.

`range` **Filter:** For matching values within a range.

`exists` **Filter:** For checking if a field exists.

`missing` **Filter (Deprecated):** For checking if a field is missing (use `must_not` with `exists` in newer versions).

3.3.3 Sorting Results:

The `sort` Parameter: Explain that the `sort` parameter is used to sort search results.

Basic Sorting: Show how to sort by a single field:

JSON

```
GET my_index/_search

{

  "query": { "match_all": {} },

  "sort": { "price": { "order": "asc" } } // Ascending order

}
```

Sorting Order (`asc, desc`): Explain the `order` parameter and its values: `asc` (ascending) and `desc`(descending).

Sorting by Multiple Fields: Show how to sort by multiple fields with different sorting orders:

JSON

```
GET my_index/_search

{

  "query": { "match_all": {} },

  "sort": [
```

```json
  { "price": { "order": "desc" } },

    { "created_at": { "order": "asc" } }

  ]

}
```

Sorting by `_score`: Explain how to sort by the relevance score (`_score`):

JSON

```
GET my_index/_search

{

  "query": { "match": { "description": "t-shirt" } },

    "sort": { "_score": { "order": "desc" } } // Sort by relevance (usually the default)

}
```

Sorting on Nested Fields: Briefly explain how to sort on nested fields (if relevant to your book's scope).

Missing Values: Explain the `missing` parameter within the sort clause that allows you to define how to handle documents where the sorting field is missing.

3.3.4 Combining Filtering and Sorting:

Practical Examples: Provide practical examples of combining filtering and sorting to refine search results based on specific criteria. For example, "find all blue t-shirts between $10 and $20, sorted by price in descending order."

By covering these points, you'll provide readers with a comprehensive understanding of how to effectively filter and sort search results in Elasticsearch. This is crucial for building user-friendly search experiences that allow users to quickly find the information they are looking for. Remember to use clear examples and code snippets to illustrate the concepts.

Chapter 4

Advanced Search Techniques

Let's break down "Boosting and Scoring for Relevance," a critical aspect of making search results useful in Elasticsearch.

4.1 Boosting and Scoring for Relevance

This section should explain how Elasticsearch calculates relevance scores and how to influence those scores using boosting.

Subsections:

4.1.1 Understanding Relevance Scoring:

TF-IDF (Term Frequency-Inverse Document Frequency): Briefly introduce the concept of TF-IDF as the foundation of Elasticsearch's scoring algorithm. Explain that:

Term Frequency (TF): How often a term appears in a document. The more often a term appears, the more relevant the document is (to a point).

Inverse Document Frequency (IDF): How rare a term is across all documents in the index. Rare terms are given more weight than common terms.

Practical Explanation: Explain TF-IDF in simpler terms, focusing on the intuition behind it: A document is more relevant if it contains the search terms frequently, especially if those terms are rare in the overall dataset.

Other Factors: Briefly mention other factors that can influence scoring, such as field length (shorter fields are often given more weight) and boosting.

`_score` **Field:** Explain that the relevance score is stored in the `_score` field of each search result.

4.1.2 Boosting at Index Time (Less Common in Elasticsearch 8):

`boost` **Parameter in Mapping (Discouraged):** Briefly mention that boosting can be applied at index time using the `boost` parameter in the mapping. However, this approach is generally discouraged in modern Elasticsearch because it's less flexible than query-time boosting.

Why It's Discouraged: Explain why index-time boosting is less flexible: It's difficult to change the boost values without reindexing all the data.

4.1.3 Boosting at Query Time (Recommended):

Boosting with the `boost` **Parameter in Queries:** Explain that the recommended way to boost is at query time, using the `boost` parameter within various queries.

Boosting with the `bool` **Query:** Explain how to use the `bool` query to boost different parts of a query:

`should` **Clause Boosting:** Explain that the `should` clause is often used for boosting optional terms. Documents that match `should` clauses will have their score increased.

Example:

JSON

```
GET my_index/_search
{
  "query": {
    "bool": {
      "must": { "match": { "description": "t-shirt" } },
      "should": [
          { "match": { "color": { "query": "blue", "boost": 2 } } } } // Boost
blue t-shirts
      ]
    }
  }
}
```

Boosting Specific Fields in `multi_match`: Show how to boost specific fields in a `multi_match` query:
JSON

```
GET my_index/_search
{
  "query": {
    "multi_match": {
      "query": "quick brown",
        "fields": ["title^3", "description"], // Boost the title field by a
factor of 3
      "type": "best_fields"
    }
  }
}
```

Function Score Query: Introduce the `function_score` query as a more advanced way to control scoring. Explain that it allows you to apply custom scoring functions based on various factors. (This might warrant a more detailed explanation in a separate advanced chapter if appropriate for your book's scope).

4.1.4 Understanding `explain`:

The `explain` Parameter: Explain the `explain` parameter, which provides detailed information about how Elasticsearch calculated the score for a particular document. This is an invaluable tool for understanding and debugging relevance issues.

Example:
JSON

```
GET my_index/_search
{
  "query": { "match": { "description": "t-shirt" } },
  "explain": true
}
```

Interpreting the `explain` Output: Show an example of the `explain` output and explain how to interpret the different parts, such as term frequencies, document frequencies, and boost values.

By covering these points, you'll provide readers with a solid understanding of how relevance scoring works in Elasticsearch and how to use boosting to influence search results. Understanding `explain` is particularly important for troubleshooting and fine-tuning relevance. Remember to use clear examples and code snippets to illustrate the concepts.

Let's break down "Fuzzy Matching and Autocompletion," two important features for improving the user experience in search applications.

4.2 Fuzzy Matching and Autocompletion

This section should explain how Elasticsearch handles fuzzy matching (finding similar terms even with typos) and how to

49

implement autocompletion (suggesting search terms as the user types).

Subsections:

4.2.1 Fuzzy Matching:

Purpose: Explain that fuzzy matching allows users to find documents even if they misspell search terms.[1]

Edit Distance: Introduce the concept of edit distance (Levenshtein distance), which measures the number of single-character edits (insertions, deletions, substitutions) required to change one word into another.[23]

Fuzziness Parameter (Revisited): Revisit the `fuzziness` parameter from the `match` query. Explain the different settings again:

`0`: Exact match only.

`1`, `2`: Allow one or two edits.

`AUTO`: Automatically determines the fuzziness based on the term length.

`fuzziness` in Other Queries: Explain that `fuzziness` can also be used in other queries like `match_phrase`, `fuzzy`, and `prefix`.

`fuzzy` Query (Direct Fuzzy Matching): Introduce the `fuzzy` query, which is specifically designed for fuzzy matching. Explain its parameters, such as `max_expansions`, `prefix_length`, and `transpositions`.

Example:

JSON

```
GET my_index/_search
{
  "query": {
    "fuzzy": {
      "description": {
        "value": "appple",
        "fuzziness": "AUTO"
      }
    }
  }
}
```

4.2.2 Autocompletion (Suggest):

Purpose: Explain that autocompletion provides search suggestions as the user types, improving the search experience and helping users find what they are looking for more quickly.

The `suggest` **API:** Introduce the `suggest` API, which is specifically designed for autocompletion and "did you mean" suggestions.

Suggesters: Explain the different types of suggesters:

`term` **suggester:** Suggests corrections for individual terms based on edit distance.

`phrase` **suggester:** Suggests corrections for entire phrases, considering word order and frequency.

`completion` **suggester:** Designed for fast and efficient autocompletion based on prefixes. This is often the best choice for autocompletion.

`completion` **Suggester in Detail:**

Mapping for `completion` **Fields:** Explain that fields intended for autocompletion need to be mapped with the `completion` type.
Example Mapping:
JSON

```
PUT my_index
{
  "mappings": {
    "properties": {
      "suggest_field": {
        "type": "completion"
      }
    }
  }
}
```

Indexing Data for `completion`**:** Show how to index data for `completion` fields:
JSON

```
POST my_index/_doc/1
{
  "suggest_field": {
    "input": ["apple iphone", "iphone 13", "apple phone"],
    "weight": 10 // Optional weight for boosting suggestions
  }
}
```

Using the `completion` **Suggester:** Show how to use the `completion` suggester in a search request:
JSON

```
GET my_index/_search
{
  "suggest": {
    "product-suggestions": {
      "prefix": "app",
      "completion": {
        "field": "suggest_field"
      }
    }
  }
}
```

Context Suggester (Optional): Briefly introduce the context suggester, which allows you to filter suggestions based on context (e.g., category, location). This can be very useful for providing more relevant suggestions.

4.2.3 Combining Fuzzy Matching and Autocompletion:

Practical Examples: Show how to combine fuzzy matching with autocompletion to handle typos in user input while providing relevant suggestions. For example, if a user types "appple", the system could still suggest "apple iphone".

By covering these points, you'll provide readers with a solid understanding of how to implement fuzzy matching and autocompletion in Elasticsearch. These features are essential for creating user-friendly and efficient search experiences. Remember to use clear examples, code snippets, and explanations to illustrate the concepts. The `completion` suggester is especially important for performant autocompletion.

Let's break down "Using Analyzers for Text Processing," a crucial topic for understanding how Elasticsearch handles text data and full-text search.

4.3 Using Analyzers for Text Processing

This section should provide a deep dive into analyzers, explaining their components and how to use them effectively.

Subsections:

4.3.1 What are Analyzers

Definition: Explain that analyzers are responsible for processing text fields both during indexing and searching. They convert text into tokens (individual words or terms) that are stored in the inverted index.[1]

The Analysis Process: Explain the three main components of an analyzer:

Character Filters: Preprocess the text by removing or modifying characters (e.g., HTML tags, punctuation).[2]

Tokenizer: Breaks the text into individual words (tokens).[3]

Token Filters: Modify the tokens (e.g., lowercase, stemming, stop word removal).[4]

Indexing vs. Search Analysis: Emphasize that the same analyzer should be used for both indexing and searching to ensure consistent results.

4.3.2 Built-in Analyzers:

`standard` **Analyzer:** Explain the default `standard` analyzer and its components:

Standard Tokenizer: Breaks text into words based on whitespace and punctuation.

Lower Case Token Filter: Converts tokens to lowercase.[5]

Stop Token Filter (Optional): Removes common words like "the," "a," and "is."[6]

`simple` **Analyzer:** Explain that the `simple` analyzer tokenizes text based on non-letter characters and lowercases the tokens.

`whitespace` **Analyzer:** Explain that the `whitespace` analyzer tokenizes text based on whitespace only.

`stop` **Analyzer:** Explain that the `stop` analyzer is similar to the `simple` analyzer but also removes stop words.

`keyword` **Analyzer:** Explain that the `keyword` analyzer treats the entire input as a single token. This is useful for fields that should not be analyzed (e.g., IDs, tags).

`pattern` **Analyzer:** Explain that the `pattern` analyzer uses a regular expression to tokenize the text.

`language` **Analyzers:** Introduce language-specific analyzers (e.g., `english`, `german`, `french`) that are optimized for different languages (stemming, stop word removal, etc.).

4.3.3 Custom Analyzers:

Defining Custom Analyzers: Explain how to define custom analyzers by combining different character filters, tokenizers, and token filters.

Structure of a Custom Analyzer: Show the JSON structure for defining a custom analyzer:

JSON

```
PUT my_index
{
  "settings": {
    "analysis": {
      "analyzer": {
        "my_custom_analyzer": {
          "type": "custom",
          "char_filter": [
            "html_strip"
          ],
          "tokenizer": "standard",
          "filter": [
            "lowercase",
            "stop",
            "porter_stem"
          ]
        }
      }
    }
  },
  "mappings": {
    "properties": {
      "my_field": {
        "type": "text",
```

```
      "analyzer": "my_custom_analyzer"
    }
  }
 }
}
```

Character Filters in Detail: Explain some common character filters:

`html_strip`: Removes HTML tags.

`mapping`: Replaces characters.

Tokenizers in Detail: Explain some common tokenizers:

`standard`: Standard tokenizer.

`keyword`: Treats the entire input as a single token.

`letter`: Tokenizes on non-letter characters.

`whitespace`: Tokenizes on whitespace.

`uax_url_email`: Tokenizes URLs and email addresses.

Token Filters in Detail: Explain some common token filters:

`lowercase`: Converts tokens to lowercase.

`stop`: Removes stop words.

`stemmer`: Applies stemming (reducing words to their root form).

`porter_stem`: Porter stemming algorithm.

`kstem`: KStem stemming algorithm.

asciifolding: Converts Unicode characters to their ASCII equivalents.

synonym: Expands tokens with synonyms.

4.3.4 Testing Analyzers:

The _analyze API: Explain how to use the _analyze API to test analyzers and see how they process text:

JSON

```
GET my_index/_analyze
{
  "analyzer": "standard",
  "text": "This is a test sentence."
}
```

or

JSON

```
  GET _analyze
{
  "analyzer": "standard",
  "text": "This is a test sentence."
}
```

Interpreting the Output: Explain how to interpret the output of the _analyze API, which shows the tokens generated by the analyzer.

By covering these points, you'll provide readers with a thorough understanding of analyzers and how to use them to effectively process text data in Elasticsearch. This is crucial for building accurate and efficient full-text search applications. Remember to use clear examples and code snippets to illustrate the concepts. Testing analyzers with the `_analyze` API is a very important practical skill.

Chapter 5

Aggregations and Analytics

Let's break down "Understanding Aggregation Framework," a powerful feature in Elasticsearch for performing data analysis and generating statistics.

5.1 Understanding Aggregation Framework

This section should introduce the Aggregation Framework, explaining its purpose, structure, and different types of aggregations.

Subsections:

5.1.1 What are Aggregations?

Definition: Explain that aggregations are a way to group and summarize data stored in Elasticsearch. They allow you to calculate metrics, create histograms, and perform other analytical operations.

Purpose: Explain why aggregations are used:

Data Analysis: To gain insights into your data.

Reporting: To generate reports and dashboards.

Business Intelligence: To make data-driven decisions.

Analogy: Compare aggregations to SQL GROUP BY and aggregate functions like COUNT, SUM, AVG, etc.

5.1.2 Aggregation Structure:

JSON Structure: Show the basic JSON structure of an aggregation request:

JSON

```
GET my_index/_search
{
  "size": 0, // We only want aggregations, not search results
  "aggs": {
    "my_aggregation_name": {
      "aggregation_type": {
        "field": "field_name"
      }
    }
  }
}
```

`size: 0`: Explain that setting `size` to 0 prevents the search results from being returned, as we are only interested in the aggregations.

`aggs` **Clause:** Explain that the `aggs` clause contains the aggregation definitions.

Aggregation Name: Explain that each aggregation has a name (e.g., `my_aggregation_name`), which is used to access the results in the response,

Aggregation Type: Explain that `aggregation_type` specifies the type of aggregation (e.g., `terms`, `histogram`, `avg`, `sum`).

Field: Explain that the `field` parameter specifies the field on which the aggregation should be performed.

5.1.3 Metric Aggregations:

Purpose: Explain that metric aggregations calculate a single value based on the data.

Common Metric Aggregations: Explain some common metric aggregations:

`avg`: Calculates the average value of a field.

`sum`: Calculates the sum of a field.

`min`: Finds the minimum value of a field.

`max`: Finds the maximum value of a field.

`count` **(Value Count Aggregation):** Counts the number of documents that have a value in a specific field.

`stats`: Calculates multiple statistics (count, min, max, avg, sum) in a single request.

`extended_stats`: Calculates additional statistics (variance, standard deviation, sum of squares).
Example:
JSON

```
GET my_index/_search
{
  "size": 0,
  "aggs": {
```

```
    "average_price": {
      "avg": {
        "field": "price"
      }
    }
  }
 }
}
```

5.1.4 Bucket Aggregations:

Purpose: Explain that bucket aggregations create "buckets" of documents based on a criteria.

Common Bucket Aggregations: Explain some common bucket aggregations:

`terms`: Creates buckets based on the terms in a field.

`histogram`: Creates buckets based on numeric ranges.

`date_histogram`: Creates buckets based on date ranges.

`range`: Creates custom numeric ranges as buckets.

`date_range`: Creates custom date ranges as buckets.

Example (`terms` aggregation):
JSON

```
GET my_index/_search
{
  "size": 0,
  "aggs": {
    "products_by_category": {
```

```
    "terms": {
      "field": "category"
    }
   }
  }
 }
}
```

5.1.5 Nested Aggregations (Sub-aggregations):

Purpose: Explain that aggregations can be nested within each other to perform more complex analysis.

Example (Combining `terms` and `avg`):
JSON

```
GET my_index/_search
{
  "size": 0,
  "aggs": {
   "products_by_category": {
    "terms": {
      "field": "category"
    },
    "aggs": {
     "average_price": {
       "avg": {
         "field": "price"
       }
     }
    }
   }
  }
}
```

5.1.6 Ordering Aggregation Results:

Explain how to order the results of bucket aggregations using the `order` parameter.

By covering these points, you'll provide readers with a solid foundation for understanding and using the Aggregation Framework in Elasticsearch. This is essential for performing data analysis and generating valuable insights from your data. Remember to use clear examples and code snippets to illustrate the concepts. The use of nested aggregations is extremely powerful.

Let's break down "Building Metrics and Statistics" within the context of Elasticsearch aggregations. This section focuses on using aggregations to derive meaningful numerical summaries from your data.

5.2 Building Metrics and Statistics

This section should dive deeper into metric aggregations and how to use them effectively to calculate various statistics.

Subsections:

5.2.1 Core Metric Aggregations (Recap and Expansion):

`avg` **(Average):** Recapitulate the `avg` aggregation and provide more practical examples. Show how to handle missing values using the `missing` parameter.

`sum` **(Sum):** Recapitulate the `sum` aggregation and provide examples.

`min` **(Minimum):** Recapitulate the `min` aggregation and provide examples.

max (Maximum): Recapitulate the `max` aggregation and provide examples.

value_count (Count): Explain the `value_count` aggregation, which counts the number of documents that have a value for a specific field. This is different from `count` within the `stats` aggregation, as `value_count` counts only documents containing a value for the specified field.

Example demonstrating `missing` parameter:

JSON

```
GET my_index/_search
{
  "size": 0,
  "aggs": {
   "average_price": {
    "avg": {
      "field": "price",
      "missing": 0 // Treat missing prices as 0
    }
   }
  }
}
```

5.2.2 Stats Aggregation:

Purpose: Explain that the `stats` aggregation calculates multiple statistics (count, min, max, avg, sum) in a single request, providing a convenient way to get a quick overview of the data distribution.
Example:

JSON

```
GET my_index/_search
{
  "size": 0,
  "aggs": {
    "price_stats": {
      "stats": {
        "field": "price"
      }
    }
  }
}
```

Interpreting the Output: Show an example of the `stats` aggregation response and explain the meaning of each field (count, min, max, avg, sum).

5.2.3 Extended Stats Aggregation:

Purpose: Explain that the `extended_stats` aggregation provides additional statistics beyond the `stats` aggregation, including:

`variance`: A measure of how spread out the data is.

`std_deviation`: The standard deviation, which is the square root of the variance.

`std_deviation_bounds`: Provides upper and lower bounds based on the standard deviation.

`sum_of_squares`: The sum of the squares of the values.

Example:
JSON

67

```
GET my_index/_search
{
  "size": 0,
  "aggs": {
   "price_extended_stats": {
    "extended_stats": {
     "field": "price"
    }
   }
  }
}
```

Interpreting the Output: Show an example of the extended_stats aggregation response and explain the meaning of the additional fields.

5.2.4 Percentiles Aggregation:

Purpose: Explain that the percentiles aggregation calculates percentiles, which are useful for understanding the distribution of data. For example, the 50th percentile (median) is the value below which 50% of the data falls.

Specifying Percentiles: Explain how to specify the percentiles to calculate:

JSON

```
MGET my_index/_search
{
  "size": 0,
  "aggs": {
   "price_percentiles": {
    "percentiles": {
     "field": "price",
      "percents": [25, 50, 75, 99] // Calculate 25th, 50th, 75th, and
99th percentiles
    }
```

```
      }
    }
}
```

TDigest Algorithm: Briefly mention that Elasticsearch uses the TDigest algorithm for calculating percentiles, which provides a good balance between accuracy and performance.

5.2.5 Cardinality Aggregation:

Purpose: Explain that the `cardinality` aggregation estimates the number of unique values in a field. This is useful for understanding the diversity of data.
Example:

JSON

```
GET my_index/_search
{
  "size": 0,
  "aggs": {
    "unique_categories": {
      "cardinality": {
        "field": "category"
      }
    }
  }
}
```

Precision Control: Briefly mention the `precision_threshold` parameter, which allows you to control the accuracy of the cardinality estimation (higher precision requires more memory).

5.2.6 Using Scripting with Metric Aggregations:

Purpose: Explain that you can use scripting within metric aggregations to perform more complex calculations.

Example: Calculating a weighted average. (Provide a simple example if appropriate for your book's scope. Scripting is often covered in more advanced chapters).

By covering these points, you'll give readers a comprehensive understanding of how to use metric aggregations to build various statistics and derive valuable insights from their data. Remember to provide clear examples, code snippets, and explanations to illustrate the concepts. The `stats`, `extended_stats`, `percentiles`, and `cardinality` aggregations are particularly useful for data analysis.

Let's break down "Creating Histograms and Buckets," focusing on bucket aggregations in Elasticsearch.

5.3 Creating Histograms and Buckets

This section should explain how to use bucket aggregations to group data into categories or ranges.

Subsections:

5.3.1 Introduction to Bucket Aggregations:

Purpose: Reiterate that bucket aggregations group documents into "buckets" based on specific criteria. This allows you to analyze data distribution and perform aggregations within each bucket.

Relationship to Metric Aggregations: Explain that bucket aggregations often work in conjunction with metric aggregations. You create buckets, and then you can calculate metrics for each bucket.

5.3.2 `terms` Aggregation:

Purpose: Explain that the `terms` aggregation creates buckets based on the terms (values) of a field. It's commonly used for categorical data.

Example: Grouping products by category:

JSON

```
GET my_index/_search
{
  "size": 0,
  "aggs": {
    "products_by_category": {
      "terms": {
        "field": "category",
        "size": 10 // Return the top 10 categories by count (default)
      }
    }
  }
}
```

`size` **Parameter:** Explain the `size` parameter, which controls the number of buckets returned.

Ordering Buckets: Explain how to order buckets using the `order` parameter. You can order by:

`_count`: The number of documents in the bucket (default descending).

`_key`: The term itself (ascending or descending).

A metric aggregation within the bucket.

Example Ordering by Count Ascending:

JSON

```
GET my_index/_search
{
  "size": 0,
  "aggs": {
    "products_by_category": {
      "terms": {
        "field": "category",
        "order": { "_count": "asc" }
      }
    }
  }
}
```

* **Example Ordering by Average Price:**

JSON

```
GET my_index/_search
{
  "size": 0,
  "aggs": {
    "products_by_category": {
      "terms": {
        "field": "category",
        "order": { "average_price": "desc" }
      },
      "aggs":{
```

```
      "average_price": { "avg": { "field": "price" } }
    }
   }
  }
}
```

min_doc_count Parameter: Explain the min_doc_count parameter, which allows you to filter out buckets with fewer than a specified number of documents.

5.3.3 histogram Aggregation:

Purpose: Explain that the histogram aggregation creates buckets based on numeric ranges (intervals).

interval Parameter: Explain the interval parameter, which specifies the width of each bucket.

Example: Creating price ranges:

JSON

```
GET my_index/_search
{
  "size": 0,
  "aggs": {
   "price_histogram": {
     "histogram": {
       "field": "price",
       "interval": 10
     }
   }
  }
}
```

min_doc_count and extended_bounds: Explain the min_doc_count (as with terms) and extended_boundsparameters (to define the minimum and maximum bounds of the histogram, even if there are no data points in those ranges).

5.3.4 date_histogram Aggregation:

Purpose: Explain that the date_histogram aggregation creates buckets based on date ranges.

calendar_interval and fixed_interval: Explain the difference between calendar_interval (which respects calendar boundaries like months and years) and fixed_interval (which uses fixed time units like milliseconds, seconds, minutes).
Example: Grouping data by month:

JSON

```
GET my_index/_search
{
  "size": 0,
  "aggs": {
    "sales_by_month": {
      "date_histogram": {
        "field": "order_date",
        "calendar_interval": "month"
      }
    }
  }
}
```

format **and** time_zone: Explain how to use the format parameter to control the date format in the bucket keys and the time_zone parameter to handle time zone conversions.

min_doc_count **and** extended_bounds: Explain the min_doc_count and extended_bounds parameters, similar to the histogram aggregation.

5.3.5 range **and** date_range **Aggregations:**
Purpose: Explain that the range aggregation allows you to define custom numeric ranges, and the date_range aggregation allows you to define custom date ranges.

ranges **Parameter:** Explain the ranges parameter, which takes an array of range definitions.

Example (range **aggregation):**
JSON

```
GET my_index/_search
{
  "size": 0,
  "aggs": {
    "price_ranges": {
      "range": {
        "field": "price",
        "ranges": [
          { "to": 20 },
          { "from": 20, "to": 50 },
          { "from": 50 }
        ]
      }
    }
  }
}
```

}

Example (`date_range` aggregation):
JSON

```
GET my_index/_search
{
  "size": 0,
  "aggs": {
   "sales_by_quarter": {
     "date_range": {
       "field": "order_date",
       "ranges": [
         { "to": "2024-04-01" },
         { "from": "2024-04-01", "to": "2024-07-01" },
         { "from": "2024-07-01" }
       ]
     }
   }
  }
 }
}
```

By covering these points, you'll provide readers with a thorough understanding of how to use bucket aggregations to group and analyze data in Elasticsearch. Remember to use clear examples and code snippets to illustrate the concepts. The use of `terms`, `histogram`, and `date_histogram` are especially important for data analysis and visualization.

Chapter 6

Working with Geospatial Data

Let's break down "Indexing Geo-Points and Geo-Shapes," covering how to work with geospatial data in Elasticsearch.

6.1 Working with Geospatial Data

This section should explain how to index and query geospatial data using Elasticsearch's geo-point and geo-shape field types.

Subsections:

6.1.1 Introduction to Geospatial Data in Elasticsearch:

Use Cases: Briefly mention common use cases for geospatial search, such as:

Finding nearby locations (e.g., restaurants, ATMs).

Geofencing (defining areas and checking if points are within them).

Location-based analytics.

Geo-Point and Geo-Shape: Introduce the two main field types for geospatial data:

`geo_point`: For representing individual points (latitude and longitude).

`geo_shape`: For representing more complex shapes (e.g., polygons, circles).

6.1.2 Indexing Geo-Points:

Mapping `geo_point` **Fields:** Explain how to map a field as a `geo_point`:

JSON

```
PUT my_index
{
  "mappings": {
    "properties": {
      "location": {
        "type": "geo_point"
      }
    }
  }
}
```

Different Formats for Geo-Points: Explain the different formats for providing geo-point data:

String: `"latitude,longitude"` (e.g., "40.712,-74.005")

Object: `{"lat": 40.712, "lon": -74.005}`

Array: `[longitude, latitude]` (e.g., [-74.005, 40.712])
Example Indexing a Geo-Point:
JSON

```
POST my_index/_doc/1
{
  "name": "Empire State Building",
  "location": "40.7484,-73.9857"
}
```

6.1.3 Querying Geo-Points:

geo_distance Query: Explain the geo_distance query, which finds documents within a specified distance of a point:
JSON

```
GET my_index/_search
{
  "query": {
   "geo_distance": {
     "distance": "1km", // Search within 1 kilometer
     "location": "40.75,-73.99" // Center point
   }
  }
}
```

geo_bounding_box Query: Explain the geo_bounding_box query, which finds documents within a rectangular area:

JSON

```
GET my_index/_search
{
  "query": {
   "geo_bounding_box": {
     "location": {
      "top_left": { "lat": 40.8, "lon": -74.1 },
      "bottom_right": { "lat": 40.7, "lon": -73.9 }
     }
   }
  }
}
```

geo_polygon **Query:** Explain the geo_polygon query, which finds documents within a polygon:

JSON

```
GET my_index/_search
{
   "query": {
     "geo_polygon": {
        "location": {
          "points": [
             [-74.0, 40.7],
             [-73.9, 40.8],
             [-73.8, 40.7]
          ]
        }
     }
   }
}
```

6.1.4 Indexing Geo-Shapes:

Mapping geo_shape **Fields:** Explain how to map a field as a geo_shape:
JSON

```
PUT my_index
{
 "mappings": {
   "properties": {
     "area": {
       "type": "geo_shape"
     }
   }
 }
}
```

}

GeoJSON Format: Explain that geo-shapes are represented using the GeoJSON format.
Example Indexing a Polygon:
JSON

```
POST my_index/_doc/1
{
  "name": "Central Park",
  "area": {
    "type": "Polygon",
    "coordinates": [
     [
       [-73.97, 40.79],
       [-73.95, 40.76],
       [-73.93, 40.80],
       [-73.97, 40.79]
     ]
    ]
  }
}
```

6.1.5 Querying Geo-Shapes:

`geo_shape` **Query:** Explain the `geo_shape` query, which allows you to perform various spatial relationships:

`intersects`: Checks if a shape intersects with the indexed shape.

`disjoint`: Checks if a shape is completely outside the indexed shape.

`within`: Checks if a shape is completely within the indexed shape.

`contains`: Checks if the indexed shape completely contains the query shape.

Example `geo_shape` **Query with** `intersects`:
JSON

```
GET my_index/_search
{
  "query": {
    "geo_shape": {
      "area": {
        "relation": "intersects",
        "shape": {
          "type": "Point",
          "coordinates": [-73.96, 40.78]
        }
      }
    }
  }
}
```

6.1.6 Geospatial Aggregations (If relevant to the book's scope):

Briefly mention geospatial aggregations, such as `geo_distance` and `geohash_grid`, which allow you to aggregate data based on location.

By covering these points, you'll give readers a solid understanding of how to work with geospatial data in Elasticsearch. This is essential for building location-based applications and performing geospatial analysis. Remember to use clear examples, code snippets, and diagrams (if applicable) to illustrate the concepts.

Let's focus specifically on "Performing Geo-Distance and Geo-Bounding Box Queries," expanding on the previous section about geospatial data.

6.2 Performing Geo-Distance and Geo-Bounding Box Queries

This section provides a more detailed look at two of the most common geospatial queries: `geo_distance` and `geo_bounding_box`.

Subsections:

6.2.1 The `geo_distance` Query:

Purpose: Clearly state the purpose: to find documents located within a specific distance from a given point.

Parameters: Explain the key parameters:

`distance`: The radius of the search area. This must be a number followed by a unit of distance (e.g., "1km", "500m", "1mi", "200yd").

`location`: The center point of the search. This can be provided in any of the `geo_point` formats (string, object, array).

`distance_type`: (Optional) Specifies how the distance is calculated. The default is `arc`, which uses a spherical model of the Earth. Other options include `plane` (a flat Earth model, faster but less accurate for long distances).

`validation_method`: (Optional) Specifies how to handle invalid geo points.

Example (Finding locations within 1km of a point):

JSON

```
GET my_index/_search
{
  "query": {
    "geo_distance": {
      "distance": "1km",
      "location": {
        "lat": 40.75,
        "lon": -73.99
      }
    }
  }
}
```

Example with `distance_type`:
JSON

```
GET my_index/_search
{
  "query": {
    "geo_distance": {
      "distance": "10mi",
      "location": [-74.006, 40.712],
      "distance_type": "plane"
    }
  }
}
```

Filtering vs. Scoring: Explain that `geo_distance` can be used in both `query` and `filter` contexts. When used in the `query` context, it calculates a score based on the distance (closer locations have higher scores). When used in the `filter` context, it simply includes or excludes documents based on whether they are within the specified distance (no scoring).

Example as a Filter:
JSON

```
GET my_index/_search
{
  "query": {
    "bool": {
      "must": {
        "match_all": {}
      },
      "filter": {
        "geo_distance": {
          "distance": "5km",
          "location": "40.7,-74"
        }
      }
    }
  }
}
```

6.2.2 The `geo_bounding_box` Query:

Purpose: Clearly state the purpose: to find documents located within a rectangular area defined by two points (top-left and bottom-right corners).

Parameters: Explain the key parameters:

`top_left` or `tl`: The coordinates of the top-left corner of the bounding box.

`bottom_right` or `br`: The coordinates of the bottom-right corner of the bounding box.

Alternatively, you can use `top_right` and `bottom_left` or `tr` and `bl`.

The coordinates can be provided in any of the `geo_point` formats.

`type`: (Optional) Can be set to `indexed` (default) or `memory`. `memory` is faster but requires more memory. Use `indexed` if you have many shapes or large shapes.

Example (Finding locations within a bounding box):
JSON

```
GET my_index/_search
{
  "query": {
    "geo_bounding_box": {
      "location": {
        "top_left": { "lat": 40.8, "lon": -74.1 },
        "bottom_right": { "lat": 40.7, "lon": -73.9 }
      }
    }
  }
}
```

Using String Format for Corners (Less Recommended): Briefly show how to use string format for defining the corners (e.g., "40.8,-74.1"), but recommend using object or array format for clarity.

Filtering vs. Scoring: Similar to `geo_distance`, explain that `geo_bounding_box` can be used in both `query` and `filter` contexts. In the `query` context it can be used to influence the score, but it's most common as a `filter`.

Example as a Filter:
JSON

```
GET my_index/_search
{
  "query": {
    "bool": {
      "must": {
        "match": { "name": "Park" }
      },
      "filter": {
        "geo_bounding_box": {
          "location": {
            "top_left": "40.78,-73.98",
            "bottom_right": "40.75,-73.95"
          }
        }
      }
    }
  }
}
```

6.2.3 Combining Geo Queries with Other Queries:

Practical Examples: Show how to combine geo_distance and geo_bounding_box with other queries (e.g., match, term, bool) to create more complex geospatial searches. For example, "find all restaurants within 500m of a specific location that serve Italian food."

By focusing specifically on these two queries and providing detailed explanations and examples, you'll give your readers a solid understanding of how to perform common geospatial searches in Elasticsearch. Emphasize the difference between using these queries in `query` vs `filter` context for performance considerations.

Let's break down "Visualizing Geospatial Data in Kibana," focusing on how to represent location-based information visually.

6.3 Visualizing Geospatial Data in Kibana

This section should guide readers through the process of creating maps and other visualizations of geospatial data using Kibana.

Subsections:

6.3.1 Connecting Kibana to Elasticsearch (Recap):

Briefly remind readers how to connect Kibana to their Elasticsearch instance. This might involve configuring the `kibana.yml` file or using the Kibana UI.

6.3.2 Creating a Map Visualization:

Opening the Maps App: Explain how to open the Maps application in Kibana.

Adding a Layer: Explain how to add a layer to the map. A layer represents a data source (an Elasticsearch index).

Choosing the Data Source: Explain how to select the Elasticsearch index containing the geospatial data.

Choosing the Geometry Field: Explain how to select the `geo_point` or `geo_shape` field that contains the location information.

Symbol Types: Explain the different symbol types that can be used to represent points on the map:

Markers: Simple icons or symbols.

Circles: Circles with a radius.

Heatmaps: Color-coded areas showing the density of points.

Styling the Map: Explain how to customize the appearance of the map, such as:

Changing the base map (e.g., road map, satellite view).

Adjusting the color and size of markers.

Adding tooltips that show information when hovering over markers.

Example (Creating a map of locations using markers): Provide step-by-step instructions with screenshots showing how to create a basic map visualization.

6.3.3 Creating a Heatmap:

Choosing the Heatmap Style: Explain how to select the heatmap style in the Maps app.

Configuring the Heatmap: Explain how to configure the heatmap, such as:

Setting the radius of the heatmap cells.

Choosing the color gradient.

Example (Creating a heatmap of crime incidents): Provide an example with screenshots showing how to create a heatmap to visualize the density of crime incidents or other similar data.

6.3.4 Creating a Region Map (using GeoJSON):

Importing GeoJSON: Explain how to import GeoJSON files into Kibana. GeoJSON files define geographical boundaries like countries, states, or postal codes.

Creating a Region Map: Explain how to create a region map using the imported GeoJSON data.

Joining Data: Explain how to join data from your Elasticsearch index with the GeoJSON data to visualize metrics for different regions (e.g., population density, sales per state).

Example (Visualizing sales by state): Provide an example with screenshots showing how to create a region map to visualize sales data by state or other geographical regions.

6.3.5 Filtering and Time-Based Filtering on Maps:

Filtering Data on the Map: Explain how to use Kibana's filtering capabilities to filter the data displayed on the map. This allows users to focus on specific subsets of data.

Time-Based Filtering: Explain how to use Kibana's time filter to visualize geospatial data over time. This can be used to create animations or see how data changes over time.

6.3.6 Using Kibana Lens for Geospatial Visualizations (If relevant):

If Kibana Lens is a core focus of your book, explain how to use it for simpler geospatial visualizations. Lens can sometimes provide a quicker way to create basic maps.

By covering these points, you'll provide readers with the practical skills to visualize their geospatial data using Kibana. This is essential for understanding patterns, trends, and insights in location-based data. Remember to use plenty of screenshots and clear step-by-step instructions to make the process easy to follow. The use of concrete examples will greatly enhance the learning experience.

Chapter 7

Managing and Monitoring Your Cluster

Let's delve deeper into "Understanding Cluster Health," a fundamental aspect of Elasticsearch cluster management.

7.1 Understanding Cluster Health

This section should thoroughly explain the concept of cluster health, how to check it, and how to interpret the results.

Subsections:

7.1.1 What is Cluster Health?

Definition: Clearly define cluster health as an indicator of the overall operational status of the Elasticsearch cluster. It reflects whether all data is available, whether redundancy is ensured, and whether the cluster is functioning as expected

Importance: Emphasize the importance of monitoring cluster health to:

Detect and address potential problems before they impact users.

Ensure data availability and prevent data loss.

Maintain optimal performance.

7.1.2 Cluster State and Metadata:

Cluster State: Explain that the cluster state is a representation of the cluster's current configuration and status. It includes information about:

Nodes in the cluster.

Indices and their settings.

Shards and their allocation.

Routing information.

Metadata: Explain that the cluster state includes metadata about the cluster, such as cluster name and version.

How Changes are Propagated: Briefly explain how changes to the cluster state are propagated to all nodes in the cluster.

7.1.3 Cluster Health Statuses (Green, Yellow, Red):

Green:

Meaning: Explain that a green status indicates that all primary and replica shards are allocated to nodes in the cluster. This means that all data is available and the cluster has full redundancy.

Implications: The cluster is operating optimally, and there are no immediate concerns

Yellow:

Meaning: Explain that a yellow status indicates that all primary shards are allocated, but some replica shards are unassigned. This means that all data is available, but redundancy is reduced. If a node containing a primary shard fails, data loss could occur.

Common Causes: Explain common causes of a yellow status, such as:

A node has recently left the cluster.

The cluster is recovering from a restart.

Insufficient resources to allocate all replicas.

Implications: The cluster is functioning, but it's important to investigate the cause of the yellow status and take corrective action to restore full redundancy.

Red:

Meaning: Explain that a red status indicates that one or more primary shards are unassigned. This means that some data is unavailable, and the cluster is partially or completely non-functional.

Common Causes: Explain common causes of a red status, such as:

A node containing a primary shard has failed.

Insufficient resources to allocate primary shards.

Index settings that prevent shard allocation.

Implications: The cluster is experiencing a serious problem that needs immediate attention to restore data availability.

7.1.4 Checking Cluster Health with the `_cluster/health` API:

Making the Request: Show how to use the `_cluster/health` API using `curl` or a similar tool:

Bash

GET _cluster/health

Parameters (Optional): Explain some useful optional parameters:

`wait_for_status`: Wait for the cluster to reach a specific status (e.g., `green`, `yellow`).

`timeout`: Set a timeout for the request.

`level`: Control the level of detail in the response (`cluster`, `indices`, `shards`).

Example with `wait_for_status` and `timeout`:

Bash
GET _cluster/health?wait_for_status=green&timeout=10s

7.1.5 Interpreting the Response (Detailed Explanation):

`cluster_name`: The name of the cluster.

`status`: The overall cluster health status (`green`, `yellow`, `red`).

`timed_out`: Indicates whether the request timed out.

`number_of_nodes`: The total number of nodes in the cluster.

`number_of_data_nodes`: The number of data nodes in the cluster (nodes that hold data).

`active_primary_shards`: The number of active primary shards.

`active_shards`: The total number of active shards (primary and replica).

`relocating_shards`: The number of shards that are currently being relocated.

`initializing_shards`: The number of shards that are currently being initialized.

`unassigned_shards`: The number of shards that are not currently assigned to a node. This is the key indicator of a yellow or red status.

`delayed_unassigned_shards`: The number of shards that are intentionally delayed from being assigned.

`number_of_pending_tasks`: The number of pending cluster-level tasks.

`number_of_in_flight_fetch`: The number of currently running shard fetch operations.

`task_max_waiting_in_queue_millis`: How long the oldest task has been waiting in the queue.

`active_shards_percent_as_number`: The percentage of active shards.

7.1.6 Practical Examples and Scenarios:
Provide realistic scenarios that illustrate how to interpret the cluster health status and take appropriate action. For example:

A node failure leading to a yellow or red status.

A rolling restart of the cluster.

Adding or removing nodes from the cluster.

By providing this detailed explanation of cluster health, you'll equip readers with the critical skills to monitor their Elasticsearch deployments and ensure their stability and reliability. Using real-world scenarios and detailed explanations of the API response will be very beneficial.

Let's make "7.3 Managing Indices and Shards" as vivid and practical as possible. Since it's a core topic for Elasticsearch administration, a deep understanding is crucial.

7.2 Managing Indices and Shards

This section empowers readers to effectively manage the core building blocks of Elasticsearch data: indices and shards.

7.2.1 Understanding Indices and Shards (A Quick Recap with Analogy):

Think of Elasticsearch as a massive library.

- **Indices:** These are like the different sections of the library (e.g., "Fiction," "History," "Science"). They logically group related books (documents). You wouldn't search for a physics textbook in the fiction section, right? Indices provide this logical separation.
- **Shards:** These are like the individual bookshelves within each section. Each bookshelf holds a portion of the books in that section. Primary shards are the original bookshelves, while replica shards are identical copies placed in different parts of the library for safekeeping (redundancy) and to allow multiple librarians to help people find books simultaneously (improved search speed).

7.2.2 Creating Indices (Detailed Configuration - Setting Up Your Library):

Creating an index is like setting up a new section in your library. You need to decide how many bookshelves you'll have (primary shards) and how many copies of each bookshelf you'll make (replica shards).

Basic Index Creation (Creating a New Section):

JSON

```
PUT my_index  // Name of the new section (index)
{
  "mappings": {
   "properties": {
      "title": { "type": "text" }, // What kind of books will this section hold? (data types)
      "author": { "type": "keyword" }
    }
  }
}
```

Settings at Index Creation (Setting Up the Bookshelves): This is where you configure the physical layout of your section.
JSON

```
PUT my_index
{
  "settings": {
    "number_of_shards": 3,      // 3 primary bookshelves
      "number_of_replicas": 1,     // 1 copy of each bookshelf (so 2 total)
      "index.refresh_interval": "1s", // How often new books become searchable
```

```
    "index.translog.durability": "request", // How carefully to record
new book arrivals
    "index.translog.flush_threshold_size": "512mb", // How full the
arrival log gets before filing it
    "index.analysis.analyzer.my_analyzer": { // Setting up a special
way to organize books
      "type": "custom",
      "tokenizer": "standard",
      "filter": ["lowercase", "stop"]
    }
  },
  "mappings": { /* ... */ }
}
```

number_of_shards **(Number of Bookshelves):** This is the *most crucial* setting. Once you set it, you *cannot change it*. Think carefully! More shelves mean faster searching and handling more books, but also more overhead to manage. A good rule of thumb is to aim for shards that are between a few gigabytes and a few tens of gigabytes in size.

number_of_replicas **(Number of Copies):** This is easy to change later. More copies mean better resilience (if a bookshelf breaks, you have a copy) and faster searching (more librarians can help).

index.refresh_interval: This determines how quickly new documents become searchable. "1s" (one second) is near real-time but can impact indexing performance. If immediate searchability isn't critical, you can increase this.

index.translog.durability: This controls how safely incoming data (new books) is recorded. request is the safest but slowest. `async` is faster but risks losing very recent data in a crash.

`index.translog.flush_threshold_size`: This controls how often the translog (a log of recent changes) is flushed to disk. Larger values improve indexing speed but increase the risk of data loss in a crash.

7.2.3 Deleting Indices (Demolishing a Section - Use with Extreme Caution!):

Bash
```
DELETE my_index      // Delete a single section
DELETE logs-*        // Delete sections starting with "logs-"
DELETE _all          // WARNING: Delete *everything*!
```

This is like demolishing a section of the library. *It's irreversible!* Use wildcards (*) with extreme caution. It's highly recommended to have backups (snapshots) in case you accidentally delete something.

7.2.4 Managing Index Settings (Fine-Tuning Your Library):
Getting Current Settings:
Bash

```
GET my_index/_settings
```

Updating Settings (Changing the Layout): You can change some settings "live" (dynamic settings), like the number of replicas or the refresh interval:
Bash

```
PUT my_index/_settings
{
  "index.number_of_replicas": 2,
```

```
  "index.refresh_interval": "5s"
}
```

Static Settings (Structural Changes): Settings like `number_of_shards` are static. To change them, you need to close the index, make the change, and then reopen it:

Bash

```
POST my_index/_close
PUT my_index/_settings { /* Change static settings here */ }
POST my_index/_open
```

7.2.5 Index Templates (Blueprints for New Sections):
Templates are like blueprints for new sections. When you create a new index that matches a template's pattern, the template's settings and mappings are automatically applied.

JSON

```
PUT _index_template/my_logs_template
{
    "index_patterns": ["logs-*"], // Applies to indices like
"logs-2024-10-26", "logs-2024-10-27", etc.
  "priority": 100, // If multiple templates match, the one with the
highest priority wins
   "template": { // This is the blueprint itself
    "settings": {
     "number_of_shards": 1,
     "number_of_replicas": 1
    },
    "mappings": {
     "properties": {
      "@timestamp": { "type": "date" },
      "message": { "type": "text" }
```

101

```
    }
  },
  "aliases": {
      "current_logs": {} // An alias that always points to the current
logs
    }
  },
  "composed_of": ["my_mappings_component"] // Use component
templates (7.8+)
}

PUT _component_template/my_mappings_component
{
  "template": {
    "mappings": {
      "properties": {
         "ip_address": { "type": "ip" }
       }
     }
   }
}
```

index_patterns: The pattern that determines which indices the template applies to.

priority: If multiple templates match, the one with the highest priority is used.

composed_of: List of component templates to include.

template: Contains the settings, mappings, and aliases to apply.

7.2.6 Managing Shards (Advanced Bookshelf Management):

Shard Allocation (Where to Put the Bookshelves): Elasticsearch automatically distributes shards across nodes. But you can control *where* they go.

Shard Allocation Filtering (Putting Bookshelves in Specific Rooms): You can use filtering to ensure shards are placed on nodes with specific characteristics (e.g., "put all fiction books in the room with the high ceilings"):

JSON

```
PUT my_index/_settings
{
  "index.routing.allocation.require.rack": "rack1" // Only allocate to nodes in "rack1"
}
```

Forced Awareness (Keeping Copies in Different Buildings): This is crucial for high availability. You can tell Elasticsearch to distribute replica shards across different racks or availability zones, so if one rack fails, you still have copies of your data. This is configured in `elasticsearch.yml` on each node.

Rerouting Shards (Moving Bookshelves Around): You can manually move shards using the `_cluster/reroute` API. This is useful for rebalancing the cluster, recovering from node failures, or performing maintenance.

JSON

```
POST _cluster/reroute?explain // Use explain to see *why* Elasticsearch is doing what it's doing
{
```

```
"commands": [
 {
  "move": {
    "index": "my_index",
    "shard": 0,
    "from_node": "node1",
    "to_node": "node2"
  }
 }
}
```

Let's craft a comprehensive section on "Performance Tuning and Optimization" for your Elasticsearch book. This is a crucial topic, as a well-tuned cluster can make a significant difference in speed and efficiency.

7.3 Performance Tuning and Optimization

This section should cover the key areas for optimizing Elasticsearch performance, both for indexing and searching.

Subsections:

7.3.1 Understanding Performance Bottlenecks:

Identifying Bottlenecks: Explain how to identify performance bottlenecks in an Elasticsearch cluster. Common bottlenecks include:

CPU Bottlenecks: High CPU utilization can indicate that the cluster is struggling to process requests.

Memory (JVM Heap) Bottlenecks: Insufficient heap size can lead to excessive garbage collection and slow performance.

Disk I/O Bottlenecks: Slow disk I/O can limit indexing and search speed.

Network Bottlenecks: Network latency and bandwidth limitations can affect communication between nodes.

Tools for Identifying Bottlenecks: Mention tools like Kibana's Monitoring UI, node statistics APIs, and system monitoring tools (e.g., `iostat`, `vmstat`, `top`).

7.3.2 Hardware Considerations:

CPU: Explain the importance of CPU performance for query processing and aggregation. More cores are generally better, especially for search-heavy workloads.

Memory (RAM): Explain the crucial role of RAM for the JVM heap and operating system caching. Sufficient RAM is essential for good performance.

Disk I/O: Explain that fast disk I/O is critical for both indexing and searching. SSDs are highly recommended.

Network: Explain the importance of low-latency, high-bandwidth network connections between nodes.

7.3.3 JVM Heap Sizing:

Importance of Correct Heap Size: Explain the importance of setting an appropriate JVM heap size. Too small a heap leads to frequent garbage collection, while too large a heap can lead to long garbage collection pauses.

Recommended Heap Size: Recommend setting the heap size to 50% of available RAM, up to a maximum of 31GB. Explain the reasons for the 31GB limit (compressed ordinary object pointers).

Setting Heap Size: Show how to set the heap size in the `jvm.options` file.

7.3.4 Indexing Performance Optimization:

Bulk Indexing (Reiterated and Expanded): Reiterate the importance of bulk indexing and provide more detailed guidelines for batch size. Recommend starting with batches of 1,000-5,000 documents and adjusting based on testing.

Refresh Interval: Explain the trade-off between near real-time search and indexing performance. Increasing the `refresh_interval` (e.g., to "30s" or even higher) can significantly improve indexing throughput.

Number of Replicas (During Indexing): Recommend setting `number_of_replicas` to 0 during bulk indexing and then increasing it after indexing is complete. This reduces the indexing overhead.

Translog Settings: Explain how to adjust the `index.translog.durability` and `index.translog.flush_threshold_size` settings to optimize indexing performance.

Disable Swapping: Explain the importance of disabling swapping to prevent performance degradation.

Optimize Mappings: Efficient mappings are essential for indexing performance. Avoid unnecessary fields and use the correct data types.

7.3.5 Search Performance Optimization:

Query Optimization: Explain how to write efficient queries. Avoid wildcard queries at the beginning of terms, use filters whenever possible, and use caching effectively.

Caching: Explain the different types of caches in Elasticsearch (e.g., node query cache, shard request cache).

Field Data Cache (for Aggregations and Sorting on Text Fields - Important Note): Explain that sorting and aggregations on `text` fields use the field data cache, which can be memory-intensive. Recommend using `keyword` fields for sorting and aggregations whenever possible. If you must use text fields, consider enabling doc values or using the `keyword` field as a sub-field of the text field.

Circuit Breakers: Explain the role of circuit breakers in preventing out-of-memory errors.

Shard Size: Explain the trade-offs of shard size. Smaller shards lead to more overhead, while larger shards can become slow to search. Aim for shards that are between a few gigabytes and a few tens of gigabytes in size.

Force Merging: Explain how to use force merging to reduce the number of segments in an index, which can improve search performance.

Pre-filtering: Filter as much as possible before performing computationally intensive operations like aggregations.

Profile API: Introduce the Profile API, which provides detailed information about query execution and can help identify performance bottlenecks in queries.

7.3.6 Monitoring and Continuous Improvement:

Importance of Continuous Monitoring: Emphasize the importance of continuously monitoring the cluster's performance and making adjustments as needed.

Iterative Tuning: Explain that performance tuning is an iterative process. You should monitor, make changes, and then monitor again to see the effect of the changes.

By covering these points, you'll provide readers with a comprehensive understanding of how to tune and optimize Elasticsearch for both indexing and searching. Remember to use concrete examples, performance benchmarks (if available), and practical advice to make this section as useful as possible. The sections on identifying bottlenecks, JVM heap sizing, and query optimization are particularly important.

Chapter 8

Security and Authentication

Okay, let's refine "8.1 Introduction to Elasticsearch Security" to be a strong opening for your security chapter.

8.1 Introduction to Elasticsearch Security

This section should set the stage for the rest of the chapter by emphasizing the importance of security and providing a high-level overview of Elasticsearch's security features.

Subsections:

8.1.1 The Critical Importance of Elasticsearch Security:

Data Sensitivity: Begin by emphasizing that Elasticsearch often stores sensitive data, including:

Personal Identifiable Information (PII)

Financial data

Log data containing sensitive information

Business-critical data

Consequences of Security Breaches: Clearly outline the potential consequences of an Elasticsearch security breach:

Data breaches and regulatory fines (e.g., GDPR, HIPAA)

Reputational damage and loss of customer trust

Business disruption and financial losses

Legal liabilities

Shared Responsibility Model: Briefly explain the shared responsibility model in cloud environments (if relevant), where the cloud provider is responsible for the security *of* the cloud, and the user is responsible for security *in* the cloud (including securing Elasticsearch).

8.1.2 Elasticsearch Security Features: A Multi-Layered Approach:

Defense in Depth: Introduce the concept of "defense in depth," which means using multiple layers of security to protect against attacks. Explain that Elasticsearch's security features provide this multi-layered approach.

Key Security Features Overview: Briefly introduce the core security features that will be covered in detail in subsequent sections:

Authentication: Verifying the identity of users and systems that are trying to access the cluster. (Think of this as checking ID cards at the library entrance.)

Authorization (Role-Based Access Control - RBAC): Controlling what actions authenticated users are allowed to perform. (Think of this as different library cards granting different access levels: some for borrowing books, some for accessing special collections.)

Encryption (Transport Layer Security - TLS): Encrypting communication between clients and the cluster, and between nodes within the cluster, preventing eavesdropping and data interception. (Think of this as sending messages in sealed envelopes.)

Auditing: Tracking security-related events, such as authentication attempts and authorization decisions, to detect suspicious activity and provide forensic information. (Think of this as keeping a log of everyone who enters and exits the library and what they do.)

IP Filtering: Restricting network access to the Elasticsearch cluster based on IP addresses. (Think of this as only allowing people from certain addresses to enter the library.)

8.1.3 Security Best Practices: The Foundation of a Secure Cluster:

Beyond Configuration: Emphasize that simply configuring the security features is not enough. Ongoing security best practices are essential.

Brief Overview of Best Practices: Briefly introduce some key security best practices that will be covered in more detail later:

Changing default passwords immediately.

Following the principle of least privilege (granting users only the necessary permissions).

Regularly patching and updating Elasticsearch.

Regular security audits and vulnerability scanning.

Network segmentation and firewall configuration.

8.1.4 Scope of this Chapter:

What Will Be Covered: Briefly state what topics will be covered in the chapter.

What Will Not Be Covered (If Applicable): Briefly mention any security-related topics that are outside the scope of the chapter (e.g., integration with external authentication systems, advanced security hardening techniques). This helps set clear expectations for the reader.

By structuring the introduction this way, you'll effectively convey the importance of Elasticsearch security and provide a clear roadmap for the rest of the chapter. The library analogy will make the concepts more relatable and easier to understand. Emphasizing the consequences of security breaches will underscore the seriousness of the topic.

Okay, here's a vivid explanation of "Implementing Role-Based Access Control (RBAC)" as subtitle two under Chapter 8 (assuming Chapter 8 is about Security), focusing on clarity, practicality, and vivid imagery:

8.2 Implementing Role-Based Access Control (RBAC)

This section dives into Role-Based Access Control (RBAC), a crucial security mechanism for managing user permissions within your Elasticsearch cluster.

8.2.1 Understanding Role-Based Access Control (The Bouncer at the Club):

Imagine your Elasticsearch cluster as a popular nightclub. RBAC is like having a bouncer at the door with a strict guest list and different levels of access.

Definition: RBAC controls access to resources (data, APIs, cluster operations) based on a user's assigned role. It's not about *who* you are (authentication), but *what you're allowed to do* (authorization).

Benefits (Why We Need a Bouncer):

Centralized Management (One Guest List): Instead of managing individual permissions for every single person trying to get in, the bouncer has one central guest list (the role definitions). This makes things much easier to manage.

Reduced Complexity (Fewer Headaches for the Bouncer): It's simpler to assign people to categories (VIP, Regular, Staff) than to remember individual preferences for everyone.

Improved Security (Keeping Out the Trouble Makers): RBAC enforces the principle of least privilege: only grant the necessary access. This minimizes the potential damage if someone's credentials are compromised.

Auditing and Compliance (Tracking Who's Inside): The bouncer keeps a log of who entered and when, which is crucial for security audits and regulatory compliance.

How RBAC Works in Elasticsearch (The Bouncer's Process):

Authentication (Checking IDs): The bouncer checks your ID to verify your identity (username and password).

Roles (The Guest List Categories): The guest list has different categories: VIPs get access to the exclusive lounge, Regulars can access the main dance floor, Staff can go behind the bar. These categories are the roles.

User-Role Assignment (Giving Out Wristbands): When you enter, you get a wristband corresponding to your category (role).

Authorization (Checking Wristbands at Each Door): Every door inside the club has a guard who checks your wristband (checks if your role has the required privileges).

8.2.2 Built-in Roles (The Master Key - Use with Extreme Caution):

Elasticsearch provides built-in roles like `superuser`, `kibana_user`, `monitor`. These are like master keys to the nightclub.

Avoid Direct Use (Except `superuser` for Initial Setup): *Never* give out master keys to regular guests (users). Only use the `superuser` role for initial setup and emergency situations. Giving everyone `superuser` access is like leaving the club doors wide open—a huge security risk.

8.2.3 Creating Custom Roles (Creating Specialized Wristbands):

Custom roles are like creating specialized wristbands for different groups of people.

Using the `_security/role` API (Defining the Wristbands):

JSON

```
PUT /_security/role/log_reader // Defining the "Log Reader" wristband
{
  "indices": [
   {
     "names": ["logs-*"], // Access to all log indices
      "privileges": ["read", "view_index_metadata"], // Can read logs and see index info
        "allow_restricted_indices": false // Cannot access system indices
    }
  ],
```

```
  "cluster": ["monitor"], // Can monitor cluster health
  "applications": [
   {
     "application": "kibana-.kibana",
     "privileges": ["read"],
     "resources": ["*"]
   }
  ],
   "run_as": [] // No impersonation allowed
}
```

indices **(Access to Specific Areas):** Defines what indices (areas of the club) the role can access.

names: The indices (e.g., `logs-*`, `products`).

privileges: What actions are allowed (`read`, `write`, `index`, `delete`, `all`). Be as specific as possible.

allow_restricted_indices: Should almost always be false.

cluster: Defines cluster-level permissions (like managing nodes or settings). Use with extreme caution.

applications: Defines application-specific permissions (like access to Kibana).

run_as: Allows a user to act as another user (impersonation). Use with caution.

8.2.4 Creating Users and Assigning Roles (Handing Out the Wristbands):

Now you create the actual people (users) and give them their wristbands (roles).

Using the `_security/user` **API (Creating the People and Giving Them Wristbands):**

JSON

```
PUT /_security/user/john_doe // Creating a user named "john_doe"
{
    "password": "SuperSecurePassword123!", // Use a strong password!
  "roles": ["log_reader"], // Giving John the "Log Reader" wristband
  "full_name": "John Doe",
  "email": "john.doe@example.com",
  "metadata": { "department": "IT" },
  "enabled": true
}
```

`roles`: Assigns one or more roles to the user.

Using `elasticsearch-users` **CLI:** A command-line tool for managing users (useful for scripting).

8.2.5 Practical Examples and Scenarios (Real-World Situations):

Security Team: Create a `security_admin` role with full access to security features and audit logs.

Application Developers: Create a `dev_team` role with write access to development indices but read access to production indices.

Kibana Dashboard Users: Create a `dashboard_viewer` role with read-only access to specific Kibana dashboards.

8.2.6 Testing Roles and Permissions (Checking If the Wristbands Work):

Using `curl` (Trying to Enter Different Areas):

Bash

```
curl    -XGET    -u    john_doe:SuperSecurePassword123!
"http://localhost:9200/logs-2024-10-28/_search" // Should work
curl    -XPOST    -u    john_doe:SuperSecurePassword123!
"http://localhost:9200/products/_doc" // Should be denied
```

Using Kibana Dev Tools (Testing Inside the Club): A convenient way to test API calls directly within Kibana.

This vivid explanation with the nightclub analogy should make RBAC much clearer and more memorable. The emphasis on practical examples and testing will help readers implement it effectively. Remember that this is now section 8.2, as you specified.

Okay, here's a refined explanation of "Securing Communication with TLS" as subtitle three under Chapter 8 (Security), using vivid analogies and focusing on practical application:

8.3 Securing Communication with TLS (Transport Layer Security)

This section explains how to encrypt communication within your Elasticsearch cluster and between clients and the cluster using TLS, ensuring data confidentiality and integrity.

8.3.1 Why TLS is Essential (The Armored Truck):

Imagine transporting valuable goods. Would you leave them exposed in the back of a pickup truck, or would you use an armored truck? TLS is the armored truck for your data, protecting it during transit.

Confidentiality (Keeping the Cargo Secret): TLS encrypts data, preventing eavesdropping. No one can see what's inside the armored truck.

Integrity (Ensuring the Cargo Arrives Intact): TLS ensures that the data hasn't been tampered with during transmission. If someone tries to open the armored truck, it will be obvious.

Authentication (Mutual TLS - Verifying Both the Sender and Receiver): In some cases, you might want both the sender and receiver to prove their identity. This is like having armed guards escorting the truck and verifying the identity of the recipient.

8.3.2 TLS Concepts (The Components of the Armored Truck):

Certificates (The Official Seal of Approval): Digital documents that verify an identity. Like an official government seal on the armored truck, indicating it's authorized.

Public and Private Keys (The Lock and Key): A pair of cryptographic keys. The public key is used to encrypt (lock) the data, and the private key is used to decrypt (unlock) it. Only the intended recipient has the private key.

Certificate Authorities (CAs - The Licensing Agency): Trusted third parties that issue certificates. Like a government agency that licenses armored truck companies.

Keystores and Truststores (The Secure Garage and Approved Recipient List): Keystores hold your private keys and certificates (your garage where you keep the truck). Truststores hold the certificates of trusted CAs (a list of approved recipients).

8.3.3 Generating Certificates (Building Your Armored Truck):

Elasticsearch provides the `elasticsearch-certutil` tool to generate certificates.

Using `elasticsearch-certutil` (Building the Truck and Getting It Certified):

Bash

```
bin/elasticsearch-certutil cert --ca elastic-ca.p12 -out elastic-certificates.p12 --name "node1"
```

This creates a certificate for "node1," signed by a CA certificate (`elastic-ca.p12`). If you don't have a CA certificate, you can create one:

Bash

```
bin/elasticsearch-certutil ca
```

Certificate Formats (PKCS#12 - The Truck's Standard Design):
Elasticsearch uses the PKCS#12 format (`.p12` or `.pfx`).

8.3.4 Configuring TLS in `elasticsearch.yml` (Setting Up the Dispatch and Receiving Points):

Configure TLS in `elasticsearch.yml` on *every node*.

YAML

```
xpack.security.transport.ssl.enabled: true  # Enable TLS for
communication between nodes (trucks)
xpack.security.transport.ssl.verification_mode: certificate # Verify
the truck's seal
xpack.security.transport.ssl.keystore.path: elastic-certificates.p12 #
Where the truck is parked
xpack.security.transport.ssl.truststore.path:  elastic-certificates.p12
# List of approved destinations
xpack.security.transport.ssl.keystore.password:      changeit      #
Password to access the garage
xpack.security.transport.ssl.truststore.password:      changeit      #
Password to access the recipient list

xpack.security.http.ssl.enabled: true  # Enable TLS for client
communication (with the outside world)
xpack.security.http.ssl.keystore.path: elastic-certificates.p12
xpack.security.http.ssl.truststore.path: elastic-certificates.p12
xpack.security.http.ssl.keystore.password: changeit
xpack.security.http.ssl.truststore.password: changeit
```

Key Settings (The Truck's Features):

`xpack.security.transport.ssl.enabled`: Enables TLS for inter-node communication.

`xpack.security.transport.ssl.verification_mode`: Enforces certificate verification.

`xpack.security.transport.ssl.keystore/truststore`: Paths to your certificates.

`xpack.security.http.ssl.enabled`: Enables TLS for client communication.

Restarting the Cluster (Dispatching the Trucks): A rolling restart is required.

8.3.5 Configuring Clients for TLS (Sending and Receiving the Cargo):

Clients need to present their own certificates or trust the server's certificate.

Using `curl` with TLS (Sending a Test Package):

Bash

curl --cacert elastic-certificates.p12 -u elastic:password "https://localhost:9200/_cluster/health"

`--cacert` specifies the trusted CA certificate.

Client Libraries (Using Specialized Delivery Services): Consult your client library's documentation.

8.3.6 Certificate Management (Maintaining the Fleet):

Key Considerations (Keeping the Trucks in Good Condition):

Certificate Expiration (Regular Maintenance): Certificates expire, plan for renewals.

Secure Storage of Private Keys (Protecting the Keys to the Trucks): Keep your private keys safe!

Using a Dedicated CA (Using a Professional Licensing Agency): Recommended for production.

By using the armored truck analogy and providing clear steps, this section should make TLS configuration more accessible and memorable. The emphasis on certificate management remains crucial. Remember this is now section 8.3.

Chapter 9

Real-World Use Cases (Part 1)

9.1 Building a Product Search Engine

Okay, let's delve into building a product search engine with Elasticsearch 8. This is a very common and powerful use case for Elasticsearch, and version 8 brings some exciting new features to the table.

Key Components and Considerations

Data Modeling:

Schema Design: How you structure your product data within Elasticsearch is crucial. You'll likely have fields like:

product_name (text, analyzed)

description (text, analyzed)

category (keyword or text with custom analysis)

brand (keyword)

price (float or scaled_float)

images (keyword or nested object for multiple images)

sku (keyword)

attributes (nested object or object with dynamic mapping for varying product specifications like size, color, etc.)

Data Types: Choosing the right data types is essential for performance and functionality. Use `keyword` for exact matching (IDs, categories), `text` for full-text search (names, descriptions), and numeric types for range queries (prices).

Indexing:

Mappings: Define mappings to control how each field is indexed and analyzed. This includes specifying analyzers for text fields to handle stemming, stop words, and synonyms.

Analyzers: Use appropriate analyzers for different fields. For example, a standard analyzer for general text, and potentially a custom analyzer for product names to handle specific naming conventions.

Index Settings: Configure index settings like the number of shards and replicas for performance and fault tolerance.

Search Queries:

Match Queries: Use `match` queries for full-text search on product names and descriptions.

Term Queries: Use `term` queries for exact matching on fields like `category` and `brand`.

Range Queries: Use `range` queries to filter products by price or other numeric attributes.

Boolean Queries: Combine multiple queries using `bool` queries with `must`, `should`, and `must_not` clauses for complex search logic.

Boosting: Use boosting to prioritize certain fields or criteria, like boosting products with higher ratings or newer arrivals.

Relevance Tuning:

Scoring: Elasticsearch uses scoring algorithms like BM25 to determine the relevance of search results. You can fine-tune scoring by adjusting parameters or using custom scoring scripts.

Synonyms: Implement synonym management to handle different ways of expressing the same concept (e.g., "shoes" and "footwear").

Stop Words: Configure stop word lists to exclude common words that don't contribute to search relevance.

Faceting and Filtering:

Facets: Use facets to provide users with filtering options based on categories, brands, price ranges, and other attributes.

Filters: Use filters to narrow down search results based on user selections.

Performance Optimization:

Caching: Utilize Elasticsearch's caching mechanisms to improve query performance.

Hardware: Choose appropriate hardware based on your data volume and query load.

Monitoring: Monitor your Elasticsearch cluster to identify and address performance bottlenecks.

User Interface:

Search Box: Implement a user-friendly search box with features like autocomplete and suggestions.

Results Page: Display search results in a clear and informative way, with relevant product information and images.

Filtering Options: Provide users with intuitive filtering options to refine their search.

Elasticsearch 8 Enhancements for Product Search

Vector Search: Elasticsearch 8 introduces native vector search capabilities, which can be used to implement semantic search. This allows users to search for products using natural language queries, rather than just keywords. This is particularly useful for product discovery and handling more complex search intents.

Dense Vector Fields: Store pre-computed embeddings of your product data (e.g., from a transformer model) in dense vector fields.

k-NN Search: Use k-nearest neighbor (k-NN) search to find products that are semantically similar to the query.

Hybrid Search: Combine keyword-based search with vector search to get the best of both worlds.

Example (Simplified Mapping)

JSON
```
{
  "mappings": {
    "properties": {
      "product_name": {
        "type": "text",
        "analyzer": "standard"
      },
      "description": {
        "type": "text",
        "analyzer": "standard"
```

```
    },
    "category": {
      "type": "keyword"
    },
    "price": {
      "type": "float"
    }
  }
 }
}
```

This is a starting point. We can go deeper into any of these areas. Do you have a specific aspect you'd like to explore further, like query examples, relevance tuning, or using vector search?

9.2 Implementing Log Analysis and Monitoring

Let's discuss implementing log analysis and monitoring with Elasticsearch 8. This is another very common and powerful use case, allowing you to gain valuable insights into your application and infrastructure performance, identify errors, and troubleshoot issues.

Key Components and Considerations

Log Collection:

Beats: Use Beats like Filebeat (for file-based logs), Metricbeat (for system and service metrics), Auditbeat (for audit logs), and Heartbeat (for uptime monitoring) to collect logs from various sources.

Logstash: For more complex log processing and enrichment, use Logstash to ingest, parse, transform, and send logs to Elasticsearch.

APM Server: For application performance monitoring, use the APM Server to collect performance data from your applications.

Data Modeling (Mapping):

Common Fields: Standardize your log data with common fields like `timestamp`, `log.level`, `message`, `service.name`, `host.name`, and `error.stack_trace`.

ECS (Elastic Common Schema): Adopting the ECS is highly recommended for consistency and compatibility with Kibana dashboards and other Elastic Stack features.

Data Types: Use appropriate data types: `date` for timestamps, `keyword` for service names and log levels, `text` for messages, and `integer` or `float` for numeric metrics.

Indexing:

Index Lifecycle Management (ILM): Use ILM to manage your indices, including rollover, shrink, and delete policies, to optimize storage and performance.

Index Templates: Define index templates to automatically apply mappings and settings to new indices based on naming patterns.

Search and Analysis:

Kibana: Use Kibana to visualize and analyze your log data with dashboards, visualizations, and the Discover app.

KQL (Kibana Query Language): Use KQL to search your logs based on keywords, fields, and operators.

Aggregations: Use aggregations to calculate metrics like counts, averages, and percentiles.

Monitoring and Alerting:

Alerting: Set up alerts in Kibana to notify you of critical events or anomalies in your logs.

Machine Learning: Use Elasticsearch's machine learning features to detect anomalies in your log data automatically.

Uptime Monitoring: Use Heartbeat to monitor the availability of your services and set up alerts for downtime.

Example Logstash Configuration (Simplified)

```
input {
 beats {
  port => 5044
 }
}
filter {
 grok {
                  match    =>    {    "message"    =>
"%{TIMESTAMP_ISO8601:timestamp}    %{LOGLEVEL:log.level}
%{GREEDYDATA:message}" }
 }
 date {
  match => [ "timestamp", "ISO8601" ]
 }
}
output {
 elasticsearch {
  hosts => ["http://elasticsearch:9200"]
  index => "logs-%{+YYYY.MM.dd}"
 }
}
```

Elasticsearch 8 Enhancements for Log Analysis

Faster Queries: Performance improvements in Elasticsearch 8 provide faster query execution for log analysis.

Improved Kibana Integration: Enhanced integration between Elasticsearch and Kibana provides a more seamless experience for log visualization and analysis.

Data Streams: Data streams simplify the management of time-series data, making it easier to ingest and query logs.

Key Use Cases

Troubleshooting: Quickly identify the root cause of application errors by searching through logs.

Performance Monitoring: Track application performance metrics and identify bottlenecks.

Security Analysis: Detect suspicious activity and security breaches by analyzing audit logs.

Compliance: Meet compliance requirements by storing and analyzing audit logs.

Example Kibana Query (KQL)

Code snippet
```
service.name : "web-server" and log.level : "error" and message : "Exception"
```

This query searches for error logs from the "web-server" service that contain the word "Exception."

We can discuss specific aspects like setting up Beats, configuring Logstash filters for different log formats, creating Kibana dashboards, or implementing alerting in more detail. What would you like to explore further?

9.3 Creating a Knowledge Base Search

Let's explore creating a knowledge base search using Elasticsearch 8. This is a valuable application for making your documentation, FAQs, and other information easily searchable for both internal teams and external users.

Key Components and Considerations

Data Ingestion:

Data Sources: Identify your knowledge base content sources: websites, wikis, documents (PDF, Word), databases, etc.

Data Extraction: Extract the relevant content from these sources. Tools like Apache Tika can help with parsing various document formats.

Data Transformation: Clean and transform the data into a suitable format for Elasticsearch. This might involve removing HTML tags, handling special characters, and splitting large documents into smaller chunks.

Data Modeling (Mapping):

Key Fields: Define the fields for your documents:

`title` (text, analyzed): The title of the document.

`content` (text, analyzed): The main content of the document.

`keywords` (keyword or text with custom analysis): Relevant keywords or tags.

`category` (keyword): Categorization of the document.

`last_updated` (date): The last update timestamp.

`url` (keyword): The URL of the original document.

Analyzers: Choose appropriate analyzers for text fields. Consider using different analyzers for `title` and `content` if necessary.

Boosting: You might want to boost the `title` field to give it more weight in search results.

Indexing:

Index Settings: Configure index settings for optimal performance.

Index Templates: Use index templates for consistent mapping and settings across indices.

Search Queries:

Match Queries: Use `match` queries for full-text search on `title` and `content`.

Multi-Match Queries: Use `multi_match` queries to search across multiple fields simultaneously.

Boosting: Use boosting to prioritize certain fields or documents (e.g., newer documents).

Fuzzy Queries: Use fuzzy queries to handle typos and misspellings.

Phrase Queries: Use phrase queries to search for exact phrases.

More Like This (MLT): Use MLT queries to find similar documents based on the content of a given document.

Relevance Tuning:

Boosting: Fine-tune boosting to achieve the desired ranking of search results.

Synonyms: Implement synonym management to handle different ways of expressing the same concept

Stop Words: Configure stop word lists to exclude common words that don't contribute to search relevance.

Faceting and Filtering:

Facets: Use facets to provide users with filtering options based on categories, keywords, or other attributes.

User Interface:

Search Box: Implement a user-friendly search box with autocomplete and suggestions.

Results Page: Display search results with relevant snippets and highlighting.

Filtering Options: Provide users with filtering options to refine their search.

Elasticsearch 8 Enhancements for Knowledge Base Search

Vector Search: Using vector search can be extremely beneficial for knowledge bases. You can embed user queries and documents into vector space and find documents that are semantically similar to the query, even if they don't share exact keywords.

Dense Vector Fields and k-NN Search: As mentioned before, store document embeddings in dense vector fields and use k-NN search for semantic similarity.

Example Mapping (Simplified)

JSON

```json
{
  "mappings": {
    "properties": {
      "title": {
        "type": "text",
        "analyzer": "standard",
        "boost": 2
      },
      "content": {
        "type": "text",
        "analyzer": "standard"
      },
      "keywords": {
        "type": "keyword"
      },
      "category": {
        "type": "keyword"
      }
    }
  }
}
```

Example Query (Multi-Match with Boosting)

JSON

```json
{
  "query": {
    "multi_match": {
      "query": "Elasticsearch performance tuning",
      "fields": ["title^2", "content"],
      "type": "best_fields"
    }
```

133

```
    }
}
```

This query searches for "Elasticsearch performance tuning" in both the `title` and `content` fields, with the `title` field having a boost of 2.

We can discuss specific aspects in more detail, such as data extraction techniques, implementing synonym management, using MLT queries, or integrating vector search. Which area would you like to explore further?

Chapter 10

Real-World Use Cases (Part 2)

10.1 Building a Geospatial Search Application

Let's discuss building a geospatial search application with Elasticsearch 8. This is a powerful way to search and filter data based on location.

Key Concepts and Considerations

Geospatial Data Types: Elasticsearch supports two main geospatial data types:

geo_point: For representing a single geographic point (latitude and longitude).

geo_shape: For representing more complex geographic shapes like polygons, lines, and circles.

Data Modeling (Mapping):

geo_point **Mapping:**

JSON

```
{
  "locatlon": {
    "type": "geo_point"
  }
}
```

You can index geo_point data in various formats:

String: `"latitude,longitude"` (e.g., "40.715,-74.009")

Object: `{"lat": 40.715, "lon": -74.009}`

Array: `[-74.009, 40.715]` (longitude, latitude)

`geo_shape` **Mapping:**

JSON

```json
{
  "location": {
    "type": "geo_shape"
  }
}
```

`geo_shape` data is typically indexed as GeoJSON.

Geospatial Queries:

`geo_distance`: Find documents within a specified distance from a point.

JSON

```json
{
  "query": {
    "geo_distance": {
      "distance": "10km",
      "location": {
        "lat": 40.715,
        "lon": -74.009
      }
    }
```

```
    }
}
```

- ○
- ○
- ○ `geo_bounding_box`: Find documents within a rectangular bounding box.
- ○ JSON

```json
{
  "query": {
    "geo_bounding_box": {
      "location": {
        "top_left": {
          "lat": 40.8,
          "lon": -74.1
        },
        "bottom_right": {
          "lat": 40.7,
          "lon": -74.0
        }
      }
    }
  }
}
```

- ○
- ○
- ○ `geo_polygon`: Find documents within a polygon.
- ○ JSON

```json
{
  "query": {
    "geo_polygon": {
      "location": {
        "points": [
```

```
      {"lat": 40.7, "lon": -74.1},
      {"lat": 40.8, "lon": -74.1},
      {"lat": 40.8, "lon": -74.0},
      {"lat": 40.7, "lon": -74.0}
    ]
  }
 }
 }
}
```

geo_shape **Queries:** Use geo_shape queries for more complex shape intersections and relationships (e.g., intersects, disjoint, within).

Geospatial Aggregations:

geo_distance **Aggregation:** Calculate statistics (e.g., counts, averages) for documents within different distance ranges from a point.

geohash_grid **Aggregation:** Create a grid of geohashes and aggregate data within each cell. This is useful for visualizing data on a map.

Performance Considerations:

Geohashes: Elasticsearch uses geohashes internally to index and search geospatial data efficiently.

Indexing Strategies: Choose the appropriate indexing strategy based on your data and query patterns.

Caching: Utilize caching to improve query performance.

Elasticsearch 8 Enhancements for Geospatial Search

Improved Performance: General performance improvements in Elasticsearch 8 also benefit geospatial queries.

Example Use Cases

Finding nearby restaurants or businesses.

Searching for properties within a specific area.

Visualizing location-based data on a map.

Tracking the movement of vehicles or assets.

Example Mapping with other fields

JSON
```json
{
  "mappings": {
    "properties": {
      "name": { "type": "text" },
      "description": { "type": "text" },
      "location": { "type": "geo_point" },
      "category": { "type": "keyword"}
    }
  }
}
```

Example Query (Finding restaurants within 5km of a locatlon)

JSON
```json
{
  "query": {
    "bool": {
      "must": [
        { "match": { "category": "restaurant" } },
```

```
{
  "geo_distance": {
    "distance": "5km",
    "location": { "lat": 34.0522, "lon": -118.2437 }
  }
}
]
}
}
}
```

This query combines a standard `match` query with a `geo_distance` query to find restaurants within 5km of Los Angeles.

We can delve into specific aspects like using `geo_shape` queries, implementing geospatial aggregations, or visualizing geospatial data in Kibana. What would you like to explore further?

10.2 Implementing a Recommendation Engine

Let's discuss implementing a recommendation engine with Elasticsearch 8. Elasticsearch isn't typically used as the sole component of a complex recommendation system (which often involves collaborative filtering, matrix factorization, etc.), but it's extremely powerful for certain types of recommendations, especially those based on user behavior and content similarity.

Approaches with Elasticsearch

Content-Based Recommendations:

Concept: Recommends items similar to what a user has previously interacted with.

Implementation:

Index items with relevant attributes (e.g., product descriptions, categories, tags).

When a user interacts with an item, use a "More Like This" (MLT) query to find similar items.

Alternatively, store user preferences (e.g., preferred categories, keywords) and use boolean queries to find matching items.

Example: A user views a science fiction book. The system recommends other science fiction books, books by the same author, or books with similar themes.

Collaborative Filtering (with limitations):

Concept: Recommends items that similar users have interacted with.

Implementation (using Elasticsearch):

Store user-item interaction data in Elasticsearch (e.g., user ID, item ID, timestamp).

Find users who have interacted with similar items as the target user.

Recommend items that these similar users have interacted with but the target user hasn't.

Limitations: Elasticsearch isn't optimized for complex collaborative filtering algorithms like matrix factorization. For large datasets and complex models, dedicated recommendation libraries (like Apache Mahout, Spark MLlib, or specialized Python libraries) are usually preferred. However, Elasticsearch can be useful for simpler collaborative filtering approaches or for pre-filtering candidates before applying more complex algorithms.

Example: Two users both purchased several fantasy novels. The system recommends a new fantasy novel to one user that the other user has already purchased.

Hybrid Approaches:

Concept: Combines content-based and collaborative filtering.

Implementation: Use Elasticsearch for content-based filtering to generate a set of candidate recommendations. Then, use other methods (or simpler Elasticsearch queries based on user interaction data) to rank or filter these candidates based on collaborative filtering principles.

Behavior-Based Recommendations:

Concept: Recommends items based on user actions within the application (e.g., views, purchases, searches).

Implementation:

Index user activity data in Elasticsearch.

Use aggregations and queries to identify patterns in user behavior.

Recommend items based on these patterns (e.g., "Customers who viewed this also viewed...").

Example: A user adds a product to their cart but doesn't complete the purchase. The system recommends that product again later.

Elasticsearch 8 Enhancements Relevant to Recommendations

Vector Search: This is a huge advancement for recommendations. By embedding items and user profiles into a vector space, you can use k-NN search to find similar items or users, enabling more nuanced and semantic recommendations.

This is especially useful for content-based recommendations and can also be used to enhance collaborative filtering approaches.

Example (Content-Based with MLT)

JSON

```json
{
  "query": {
    "more_like_this": {
      "fields": ["description", "title"],
      "like": [
        {
          "_index": "products",
          "_id": "123" // ID of the product the user interacted with
        }
      ],
      "min_term_freq": 1,
      "min_doc_freq": 1
    }
  }
}
```

Example (Hybrid Approach - Content-Based pre-filtering with user category preference)

JSON

```json
{
  "query": {
    "bool": {
      "must": [
        {
          "more_like_this": {
            "fields": ["description", "title"],
            "like": [
              {
```

```
          "_index": "products",
          "_id": "123"
        }
      ]
    }
  },
  {
    "term": {
      "category": "Science Fiction" // User's preferred category
    }
  }
]
      }
    }
  }
}
```

Key Considerations:

Data Volume: Elasticsearch is well-suited for handling large volumes of data.

Performance: Optimize queries and indexing for fast response times.

Relevance Tuning: Fine-tune scoring and boosting to improve the quality of recommendations.

Cold Start Problem: This is a common challenge in recommendation systems. When a new user or item has very little interaction data, it's difficult to provide relevant recommendations. Consider using default recommendations or content-based approaches to address this.

We can discuss specific aspects like implementing vector search for recommendations, handling the cold start problem, or combining Elasticsearch with other recommendation libraries. What would you like to explore in more detail?

10.3 Building a Site Search for a Large Website

Let's discuss building a site search for a large website using Elasticsearch 8. This is a critical feature for user experience, allowing visitors to quickly find the information they need.

Key Considerations and Components:

Content Crawling and Indexing:

Web Crawlers: Use a web crawler (like Apache Nutch, Scrapy, or commercial crawlers) to gather content from your website.

Data Extraction: Extract relevant content (text, metadata, images) from web pages. Consider using libraries like Beautiful Soup (Python) or similar tools for parsing HTML.

Data Transformation: Clean and transform the extracted data into a format suitable for Elasticsearch. Remove HTML tags, handle special characters, and potentially segment large pages into smaller, more manageable chunks.

Indexing: Index the extracted data into Elasticsearch.

Data Modeling (Mapping):

Key Fields: Define relevant fields:

`title` (text, analyzed, boosted): The page title.

`content` (text, analyzed): The main content of the page.

`url` (keyword): The URL of the page.

`meta_description` (text, analyzed): The meta description of the page.

`keywords` (keyword or text with custom analysis): Meta keywords or tags.

`last_modified` (date): The last modification date of the page.

`content_type` (keyword): The type of content (e.g., page, blog post, product page).

`category` or `tags` (keyword or nested): Categorization or tagging of the page.

Analyzers: Choose appropriate analyzers. Consider using different analyzers for different fields (e.g., a more aggressive analyzer for the `content` field and a more precise analyzer for the `title` field).

Boosting: Boost important fields like `title` and `meta_description` to give them more weight in search results.

Search Queries:

`multi_match` **Queries:** Use `multi_match` queries to search across multiple fields simultaneously.

Boosting: Use boosting to prioritize certain fields or content types.

Fuzzy Queries: Use fuzzy queries to handle typos and misspellings.

Phrase Queries: Use phrase queries for exact phrase matching.

Prefix Queries: Use prefix queries for autocomplete functionality.

Boolean Queries: Combine multiple queries using `bool` queries for complex search logic.

Relevance Tuning:

Boosting: Fine-tune boosting to achieve the desired ranking.

Synonyms: Implement synonym management.

Stop Words: Configure stop word lists.

Query Rewriting: Use query rewriting techniques to improve search accuracy

Faceting and Filtering:

Facets: Use facets to allow users to filter results by category, content type, date, or other attributes.

User Interface:

Autocomplete/Suggestions: Implement autocomplete and search suggestions to improve the search experience.

Highlighting: Highlight search terms in the results snippets.

Pagination: Implement pagination for large result sets.

"Did you mean?" Suggestions: Provide "Did you mean?" suggestions for misspelled queries.

Elasticsearch 8 Enhancements:

Vector Search: Enables semantic search, allowing users to search using natural language or concepts, rather than just keywords. This can significantly improve search accuracy and user experience

Improved Performance: Performance improvements in Elasticsearch 8 enhance query speed and scalability, crucial for large websites.

Example Mapping (Simplified):

JSON
```
{
  "mappings": {
    "properties": {
      "title": {
        "type": "text",
        "analyzer": "standard",
        "boost": 3
      },
      "content": {
        "type": "text",
        "analyzer": "standard"
      },
      "url": {
        "type": "keyword"
      },
      "category": {
        "type": "keyword"
      }
    }
  }
}
```

Example Query (Multi-Match with Boosting and Fuzzy Matching):

JSON
```
{
  "query": {
```

```
  "multi_match": {
    "query": "elasticsearch tutorial",
    "fields": ["title^3", "content", "meta_description^2"],
    "fuzziness": "AUTO"
  }
 }
}
```

This query searches for "elasticsearch tutorial" across the `title`, `content`, and `meta_description` fields, with boosting and fuzzy matching enabled.

Scaling for Large Websites:

Sharding and Replication: Properly configure sharding and replication for performance and fault tolerance

Hardware: Use appropriate hardware based on data volume and query load.

Monitoring and Logging: Monitor your Elasticsearch cluster and application logs to identify and address performance issues

Caching: Utilize Elasticsearch's caching mechanisms and consider implementing a caching layer in your application.

We can discuss specific aspects like crawling strategies, implementing autocomplete, using vector search, or optimizing performance for high traffic. What would you like to explore further?